Acclaim for **STEPHE**

D0546736

Holy C_____

"Stephen Kendrick is a great friend both to the mystery writer and the seeker after spiritual truth by reintroducing us to each other—or to that other half of ourselves—so that we see anew our lifelong alliance and our brotherhood in the joy of the search.
—Anne Perry, author of *A Breach of Promise* and *Brunswick Gardens*

"Kendrick's lively readings of the Sherlock Holmes stories [show] a deep sense of how attentiveness to the details of ordinary life can yield extraordinary insights into the life of the spirit."
—*Publishers Weekly*

"*Holy Clues* is a delightful and elegant job of theological detective work. Holmes himself would be proud—and so would C. S. Lewis!" —Dan Wakefield, author of *Returning*

"Even irreligious Sherlockians should find Kendrick's book intriguing."
—*Booklist*

"Ingenious and fascinating. . . . I cannot overpraise the charm and wisdom of this book."
—Frederick Buechner, author of *The Longing for Home* and *The Storm*

"Kendrick breaks Holmes's most important code. If you want to grow spiritually and have fun at the same time, curl up and enjoy this gentle tour de force."
—Forrest Church, author of *Life Lines*

STEPHEN KENDRICK

Holy Clues

Stephen Kendrick is the Parish Minister of the Universalist Church of West Hartford, Connecticut, and has previously served churches in Maryland and Pennsylvania and Unitarian chapels in the West Midlands of England. He received his B.A. from Princeton, his M.Div. from the Harvard Divinity School, and a master's degree in creative writing from the Hollins College Writing Program. His articles have appeared in *The Christian Century, The Hartford Courant, The Hartford Advocate,* and *The New York Times.* He lives in West Hartford.

HOLY CLUES

HOLY CLUES

*The Gospel According
to Sherlock Holmes*

STEPHEN KENDRICK

VINTAGE BOOKS

A Division of Random House, Inc.

New York

FIRST VINTAGE BOOKS EDITION, JULY 2000

Illustrations are by Sidney Paget and originally appeared in *The Strand*
magazine of London.

Grateful acknowledgment is made to the following for permission to
reprint previously published material: *Estate of Dame Jean Conan Doyle:*
Excerpts from *Sherlock Holmes Stories*. Copyright © by the Estate of
Dame Jean Conan Doyle. Reprinted by permission of the Estate of Dame
Jean Conan Doyle. *Harvard University Press:* Excerpt from poem #338
from *The Poems of Emily Dickinson*, edited by Thomas H. Johnson
(Cambridge, Massachusetts: The Belknap Press of Harvard University
Press). Copyright © 1951, 1955, 1979, 1983 by the President and Fellows
of Harvard College. Reprinted by permission of the publishers and the
Trustees of Amherst College.

The Library of Congress has cataloged the Pantheon edition as follows:
Kendrick , Stephen, 1954–
Holy clues : the Gospel according to Sherlock Holmes / Stephen Kendrick.
p. cm.
ISBN 0-375-40366-3
1. Detective and mystery stories, English—History and criticism.   2. Doyle,
Arthur Conan, Sir, 1859–1930—Characters—Sherlock Holmes.   3. Religious
fiction, English—History and criticism.   4. Holmes, Sherlock (Fictitious
character)   5. Mysticism in literature.   6. Religion and literature.   I. Title.
PR830.D4K46 1999
823'.8—dc21 98-49094
CIP

Vintage ISBN: 0-375-70338-1

Author photograph © Christine Breslin

www.vintagebooks.com

Printed in the United States of America
10   9   8   7   6   5   4   3   2   1

For my parents:

A. T. Kendrick

and

Kathryn Byrd Kendrick

Verily thou art a God
that hidest thyself.

—Isaiah 45:15

"You know my methods.
Apply them."

—Holmes to Watson,
The Sign of Four

CONTENTS

HOLY CLUES

INTRODUCTION ✳ *Spiritual Fingerprints*

"WE REACH, WE GRASP, AND WHAT IS LEFT IN OUR HANDS IN THE
END? A SHADOW."

"YOU SEE, BUT YOU DO NOT OBSERVE."

"IT IS MY BUSINESS TO KNOW WHAT OTHER PEOPLE DON'T
KNOW."

THESE ENIGMATIC PHRASES could easily come from some
exalted spiritual teacher—imparted perhaps by some Eastern guru, or maybe a mystical priest, but certainly from a
sage trying to shake listeners free from their everyday perceptions. These are utterances from someone inviting you
into the mysteries of the spirit.

In fact, these are the words of Mr. Sherlock Holmes, the
world's first and most famous private consulting detective,
of 221-B Baker Street, London.

A strange religious sage, this unemotional, logical man!

Even Dr. Watson, the detective's trusted friend, admitted
that Holmes seemed to be immune to sensitive feelings of
any sort. Thoughts of love, in particular, were "abhorrent to
his cold, precise but admirably balanced mind. He was, I take
it, the most perfect reasoning and observing machine that
the world has seen. . . ."

Yet not all is as it appears on the surface. It never is, in
a proper mystery. As Holmes says, "These are very deep
waters."

Now, it is true that Holmes is presented as being thoroughly skeptical, totally immune to the lure of the super-natural; and that he and Watson are never shown once in fifty-six stories and four novels ever attending a worship service or showing the slightest interest in organized religion; and even true that Holmes admits at the conclusion of "The Crooked Man" that his knowledge of the Bible is "a trifle rusty." (Nevertheless, his remembering the sexual secret in the story of David and Bathsheba in "first or second Samuel" allows him to solve the case.)

Despite all this, there is a religious teacher here, and a deeply wise one at that. And beyond this, in these long-popular mysteries, there are many powerful clues to a higher mystery, a mystery we at last all share. As Albert Schweitzer said, "Whenever we penetrate to the heart of things, we always find a mystery. Life and all that goes with it is unfathomable. . . ."

On the surface, the Sherlock Holmes mysteries do seem to be singularly unlikely guides to ineffable secrets of life. Still, I have discovered in them an intriguing gateway to understanding something quite surprising: that detective stories of all kinds may be seen as subtly humble religious parables. After all, if the sleuth can discover the darkest and most guarded and protected secrets within the human heart, can that of God's inscrutable will be far behind? Perhaps, at last, they are the same mystery.

RELIGION AND DEDUCTION—AN EXACT SCIENCE?

It may be many years since you have picked up a Sherlock Holmes story. Yet it is very likely that, at some time in our lives, we have all joined Holmes in his search for the elusive truth in so many guises: stolen jewels, a spectral hound on the misted moors of Devon, a missing royal crown, the secret identity of a man who writes in blood on walls.

We have gone with Holmes as he moves through the yellow-fogged London of our imaginations. We think we know exactly who he is, this omnipresent and mythical figure: angular, intense, eyes fiercely aglow with the excitement of the chase. He is somehow known to all of us, the primal pursuer of disguised truth. Yet there is so much in Holmes that we have never noticed before—almost a secret identity.

He is more than simply a bloodhound of justice, as we see in a seldom-noticed moment in "The Naval Treaty," when Holmes languidly picks up a rose and takes a deep whiff as he leans on a windowsill. "There is nothing in which deduction is so necessary as in religion. It can be built up as an exact science by the reasoner." Religion! This, from one who presents himself as the scoffer, the eternal skeptic.

This astonishing statement, so atypical of Holmes, the archetype of the cold analytical detective, opens to this further rumination: "Our highest assurance of the goodness of Providence seems to me to rest in the flowers. All other things, our powers, our desires, our food, are really necessary for our existence in the first instance. But this rose is an extra. Its smell and its color are an embellishment of life, not a condition of it. It is only goodness which gives extras, and so I say again that we have much to hope from the flowers."

Yes, Holmes is an unusual spiritual sage, but truth sometimes comes to us in odd packaging. It can even come in such a lowly guise as detective fiction, despised by critics and overlooked as mere puzzle-mongering.

This book will try to reveal what Holmes means when he

says there is "nothing in which deduction is so necessary as in religion." The game's afoot, to quote the Master, and the quarry is the divine.

Holmes is more than a literary detective—he is one of the greatest fictional characters ever devised. He is more than a great fictional character—he is, quite literally, a legend.

G. K. Chesterton, who created, in the meek Father Brown, one of the few detectives who can conceivably be ranked with Holmes, wrote in admiration, "Mr. Conan Doyle's hero is probably the one literary creation since the creations of Dickens which has really passed into the life and language of the people, and became a being like John Bull or Father Christmas." Chesterton went so far as to urge that Sherlock Holmes needed a statue in London, since the only equivalent twentieth-century literary legend, Peter Pan, already had one!

But modern London cannot contain Holmes—he lives on, instead, in a realm beyond geography and place, a timeless, fog-bound London of our imagination, lit by gaslight and dreams. This extravagant popular love affair with Holmes is not something that evolved slowly. Once the *Strand* magazine started running short stories about "the world's first consulting detective" in 1891, there was an immediate explosion of interest in Holmes. This public obsession continued for over forty years, causing Conan Doyle untold distress because he believed, rightly, that these detective tales were obscuring his other, more "serious" work, especially, as we shall see, his religious life expressed in Spiritualism.

In fact, Doyle intended to write only six adventures of a figure he first called Ormond Sacker, but Doyle, a competent but unsuccessful doctor, was prevailed upon to write six more. When these stories were published together

as *The Adventures of Sherlock Holmes* in 1892, Doyle hoped to close down the series, but his mother, his editor, and countless readers demanded more. To his suggestion that "I think of slaying Holmes in the last and winding him up for good and all, He takes my mind from better things," his mother wrote back with keen editorial judgment: "You won't! You can't! You mustn't!"

Thinking no sane person would pay it, Doyle asked for a thousand pounds for more Holmes stories, and he was immediately taken up on the offer. So, in the 1892 Christmas issue of the *Strand*, new adventures began to appear; and yet, determined to ease Holmes out of his life forever, Doyle titled the last "The Final Problem." To this end, Doyle devised the ultimate plot device: someone who could credibly be matched against the intellect, though not the morals, of Holmes. It would be the master criminal Professor James Moriarty who would take the sleuth, literally, to the brink of oblivion. Down Holmes and Moriarty went into the churning waters and deadly rocks at the base of the two-hundred-foot-high Reichenbach Falls in Switzerland. In this story, Watson sadly records the demise of "the best and the wisest man I have ever known."

It is said young men wore black armbands when Doyle sent his most popular character over the falls, and that all

England mourned his presumed death. Of course, Doyle, not being a fool, never revealed Holmes's dead body, and since, despite all his annoyance with Holmes, the good detective had, effectively, bankrolled all his other work, a resurrection was always waiting in the wings.

After eight years, with "The Adventure of the Empty House," Holmes finally reappeared in the flesh. (*The Hound of the Baskervilles,* published in 1902, during that long dry interval, to rapturous reviews and critical acclaim, had been slyly presented as a case from the past.) After this, no one took Doyle's protests seriously again, with more stories appearing infrequently until, with the 1927 publication of *The Casebook of Sherlock Holmes,* Doyle finally, more than thirty years later, freed himself of the protean figure of his own creation.

Holmes was here to stay, even when his creator died, as mortals do, in 1930. So the saga continues, surprisingly, to this day. No one really believes that people read and reread these tales, nearly a hundred years on, merely for the resolution of each puzzle.

We go back again and again to witness the wonderfully evocative Victorian scenes of an England long swept away not merely by time, but by the twin cataclysms of two world wars; to experience the warm and occasionally comic scenes of friendship between the long-suffering Watson and his odd and exasperating friend; and, above all, to feel the strange allure of Holmes himself.

Yet why are we so devoted to a figure like Holmes?

Because there are qualities about this seeker that make him eternally fascinating. He teaches us to *see,* to truly observe the world. In dozens of dialogues with his "student," Watson, over and over Holmes attempts to awaken in his friend the skills and the willingness to see things as they are, not as one wishes, believes, projects, or fantasizes they are. As Wittgenstein said, in a Zen-like fashion much like Holmes's, "Don't think. Look!" This is harder to do than it might seem, harder than we can practice, and it takes patience and a good teacher. As one Buddhist teacher a long time ago put it, "The foolish reject what they see, not what they think. The wise reject what they think, not what they see." There will be many a case that turns on Holmes's ability to simply gaze at a crime scene and see it without prior theories or prejudice, to see what is really present. Keeping perception clear is the opening to insight.

Moreover, his devotion to the truth makes Holmes more than merely a man to admire; it somehow elevates him to being a new kind of monk who offers his life for others. Doyle has constructed a character who, despite evident flaws, nevertheless possesses a nearly superhuman vision into the moral life of all those he meets.

The woman who comes to seek Holmes's help in "The Speckled Band," Helen Stoner, says, "But I have heard, Mr. Holmes, that you can see deeply into the manifold wickedness of the human heart." So he does, and such is his devotion to the truth that we trust him never to be corrupted by what he sees. This passion is more than admirable, it is nearly holy. When Holmes says, the evening before he faces his archenemy, Professor Moriarty, above the treacherous Reichenbach Falls, "In over a thousand cases I am not aware that I have ever used my powers on the wrong side," we sense that he is stating the truth, not making a vain boast.

Yes, Holmes possesses a powerful moral grandeur, but is he thus a religious figure? Why should we consider him at all in the realm of things spiritual?

For those who say mystery stories can tell us nothing about spirituality, I refer back to the opening pages of Genesis (4:1–16), where murder enters history—almost as soon as life begins—outside of the ideal Garden of Eden. Cain and Abel are the first children in human history, and already, as God says, "sin is crouching at the door." When the Lord spurns the grain sacrifices of Cain and accepts the meat sacrifices of Abel, Cain invites his brother into a field and, filled with a jealous rage, kills him.

After this first murder, God comes to ask, "Where is Abel, thy brother?" Cain replies with one of the most famous evasions ever: "I know not: am I my brother's keeper?"

It is not too much of a stretch to say, only four lessons into the Bible, that God is revealed as the first detective. He certainly assigns guilt, by proclaiming to Cain, "What hast thou done?" And the reason God knows the murderer?

The most primal clue of all—the evidence of spilled blood: "The voice of thy brother's blood crieth unto me from the ground."

Is this not what every detective confronts before the dreadful reality of murder? There is always the hope that the evidence will indeed cry out who is the guilty one. Death always leaves its traces, and so it is in *Genesis* and beyond. The detective who searches for evidence that can cry out "Guilt!" is simply acting out God's role so early in the first book of the Bible.

In his book *Mysterium and Mystery—The Clerical Crime Novel,* which details the scores of fictional religious figures who have also been detectives, William David Spencer makes the astonishing statement, "In one very real sense the story of Jesus is a murder mystery." He sees the classic structure: Jesus as victim, humanity as killer, God (as we have just seen, above) as judge. "The quest of the theologian for the truth about Christ begins like the search of the detective for the mystery of evil. . . . If some Christians question whether a mystery story can be a Christian story, they do not know their own faith thoroughly enough."

Recently, I was surprised to find in a serious guide to great spiritual writings a whole chapter devoted to detective novels! Eugene Peterson, its editor, wonders why clergy are attracted to detective stories, which are always, so unlike our own experience, neatly solved by the last page. Perhaps, he guesses, it is because clergy "spend most of their time with sinners of every conceivable variety. Some of them are quite ready to confess their sins; but concealment is also practiced extensively. Because their life experience immerses them in the vagaries of sin, men and women in holy orders are splendidly qualified for detecting it." But there is something more here than simple entertainment. This connection between detection and faith goes back a long way.

In the 1930s, when early critics of detective fiction were trying to give the form some credibility and luster, several (including the great Golden Age creator of Lord Peter Wimsey, Dorothy L. Sayers), pointed out that two books in the Apocrypha, Bel and The Dragon and Susannah, both feature a kind of early detective in a young man named Daniel. In one, Daniel exposes the machinations of the priests of Bel, and in the other, he questions the elders who lie about Susannah's virtue. Simple as they are, they are undeniably precursors of the modern detective story.

As the young girl Susannah is falsely accused, Daniel cries, "Are you such fools, sons of Israel? Without questioning or finding out plainly, you sentence to death a daughter of Israel? Now separate them a distance from one another for me so that I may cross-examine them." He then shrewdly uses deduction and cross-referencing to expose false testimony and uncover corruption.

God, in these instances, seems to move through the figure of Daniel to stand with the oppressed and those treated unjustly. These biblical books from the Apocrypha may not be well known, but they stand as evidence that deduction is clearly in the Jewish and Christian tradition.

THE DETECTIVE ENTERS THE RITUAL

Certainly many mystery writers see a religious dimension to their trade. P. D. James, whose *A Taste for Death* is an explicitly religious tale while still obeying all the rules of detective fiction, says, "The mystery's very much the modern morality play. You have an almost ritual killing and a victim, you have a murderer who in some sense represents the forces of evil, you have your detective coming in—very likely to avenge the death—who represents justice, retribution." This observation is backed up by the dozens of detective novels with clerical detectives, from the famous Father Brown stories of the 1920s to today's Rabbi Small mysteries. In fact, I have collected over three hundred clergy detective novels—almost a genre in itself! But the detective does not have to wear a collar or ecclesiastical garb to have a subtle religious undercurrent moving through the investigation.

The English poet laureate C. Day Lewis, who under the nom de plume Nicholas Blake wrote many detective novels, once wondered if the decline of religious myths in our time could serve to explain the tremendous popularity of murder fiction. He fantasized some future anthropologist studying us: "When a religion has lost its hold upon men's hearts, they must have some other outlet for the sense of guilt. . . . He will call attention to the pattern of the detective novel, as highly formalized as that of a religious ritual, with its initial necessary sin (the murder), its victim, its high priest (the criminal) who must in turn be destroyed by a yet higher power. . . ." Thus the detective enters the ritual. Lewis even likened the typical close of a detective story to a kind of final Day of Judgment, wherein the mystery is revealed and the guilty separated from the innocent.

My task is simpler. Some years ago, several people in one week of counseling had asked me, "Where is God in all this pain/mess/hopelessness?" These are not easy queries, and it is easy to be weary when too many questions pile up on your soul. So in response, I wrote what I thought was a light, whimsical sermon called "The Case of the Missing God," using the Sherlock Holmes stories I had loved for so many years as a frame for the search.

To my surprise, people in the congregation thought I was on the trail of something. When I encountered these haunting words from Franz Kafka, I realized exactly why this light sermon about the search for God had struck such a nerve: "Everyday life is the greatest detective story ever written. Every second, without noticing, we pass by thousands of corpses and crimes. That's the routine of our lives."

Maybe people read detective fiction for the same reason they adopt religious doctrine. We all desperately crave both internal order and cosmic understanding: a sense that there is a hidden force operating through and beneath us that makes life not only sensible and just but, more importantly, reveals compassion at the heart of creation.

A minister is not a detective, but I admit I sometimes feel

13

like one, looking out at my congregation on a typical Sunday morning. Why is that person silently weeping? What secret does she conceal beneath her placid exterior?

Where did that boy's bruise come from—the playground or a parent's hand?

Why is that older member looking so pale and drawn—the aftermath of flu or a devastating diagnosis of cancer?

I know I will learn only a fraction of the truths in these people's lives, and that these confidences should only be given and shared in love, not arrived at by means of cold deduction. I have no right to probe or to deduce, but I also know there are important mysteries beneath the surface of these lives, and that does not even include the more traditional questions of faith people normally think to bring to their pastor:

What is the meaning of my life?

Is there a God who cares whether I live or die?

Is death the end of my story?

And so we gently ask, "How are you doing? How are things going for you?" because the divine secret within each of us is indeed the greatest detective story ever written.

THE SEARCH FOR A BLACK CAT IN A BLACK ROOM

The clues are scattered all about us. God's fingerprints are everywhere.

Yet our search for God can become frenzied, fierce, and all-consuming, as if the mystery of the divine could be solved like a cheap mystery novel where all the clues come together in the last five pages. I heard a joke years ago, when I was a student at the Harvard Divinity School, which just happens to be separated by a parking lot from both the Harvard Physics Cyclotron and the Biology Labs Recombinant DNA research labs, so the joke made a kind of bitter sense.

It seems a scientist, a philosopher, and a theologian were comparing the difficulties of their tasks. The scientist said, "I think our search for final answers resembles someone searching for a black cat in a black room, but with a flashlight."

The philosopher conjectured, "Our task is more like searching for a black cat in a black room, even without the light."

They turned to the theologian, who smiled. "I'd say we theologians are searching for a black cat, in a black room, without a light, and with no life in the room—and finding it!"

There's nothing new to this, of course. God, the "black cat" of all human searching, has been found and found again by many who have chosen to speak with confidence and surety. If the Bible teaches us anything, it is that this mystery has not changed a whit across the thousands of years, nor has human nature. One of the comforters of Job said to the tormented man sitting in the ashes of his life (11:5–8): "But, oh, that God would speak, and open his lips to you, and that he would tell you the secrets of wisdom! . . . Can you find out the deep things of God? Can you find out the limit of the Almighty?" In other words, the mystery of Job's suffering is beyond solution.

Yet we never stop searching for these "deep things." But what does Mr. Sherlock Holmes search for? None of Holmes's cases are seemingly religious on the surface, though, as we shall see, some touch on the seemingly supernatural, while others concern ecclesiastical figures. At least twice Watson drops references to Holmes's employment by the Pope himself. In Holmes's modest words, he was "exceedingly preoccupied by that little affair of the Vatican cameos." He must have satisfied Pope Leo XIII, because Watson later refers to an investigation into "the sudden death of Cardinal Tosca."

The Pope might not have appreciated Holmes's ambivalent reply to Watson in the first chapter of *The Valley of Fear*, when they are trying to solve a complicated code in a letter nervously sent by one of Moriarty's minions. They need to discover what two-columned book might be the key to the code. It is a long book, and one the writer assumes would be easily close at hand. Holmes urges Watson for one more "brain-wave."

"The Bible!" Watson cries triumphantly.

"Good, Watson, good! But not, if I may say so, quite good enough! Even if I accepted the compliment for myself, I could hardly name any volume which would be less likely to lie at the elbow of one of Moriarty's associates." We are left by this comment unsure if Holmes even owns a Bible!

The only clear religious interest on the part of Holmes we are ever given presents him as an eclectic religious searcher, especially concerning the religions of the East. This interfaith curiosity is signaled early, when, during a lull in the investigation of *The Sign of Four*, Holmes is chatting away with casual brilliance on many subjects, "on miracle plays, on mediaeval pottery, on Stradivarius violins, on the Buddhism of Ceylon, and on the warships of the future." Watson adds that he spoke "as though he had made a special study of it."

That Holmes would study Hinayana Buddhism seems surprising, but when one examines the ancient sources of this rigorous minority branch of Buddhism, the attraction becomes clear. Hinayana Buddhism claims to be the oldest and most accurate account of the teachings of the Buddha and presents its teacher as a figure who is cool, rational, and emotionally distant. The Compassionate Buddha of Mahayana Buddhism is not yet developed. Hinayana Buddhism is the branch of the religion that stresses personal effort to find nirvana, and the Buddha is a strict and intellectually rigorous instructor. You can quickly see the attraction to a man as cold and emotionally constrained as Holmes. In "The Veiled Lodger," Watson describes his friend as sitting "upon the floor like some strange Buddha, with crossed legs. . . ."

That this interest in Eastern religion and Buddhism is not idle is demonstrated by Holmes's activities during his three-year "hiatus," when he was considered a dead man, free to do and go as he pleased. The world, including Watson, thought he was at the bottom of the Reichenbach Falls along with Professor Moriarty. And how did Holmes choose to spend his new life? He exploited his freedom from the public eye in a telling way.

For two of those years he traveled in Tibet, and, as he put it later, "amused myself by visiting Lhassa, and spending some days with the head lama." (Doyle, in the first version of this story, "The Empty House," actually spelled the head of Tibetan Buddhism as "llama," which might indicate either Holmes actually visited the Andes mountains in Chile or that his personal knowledge of Buddhism did not include a dictionary!) Holmes is never more Britishly understated than when he uses the term *amused*, especially as no Westerner had to that time been able to penetrate the harsh climes and the inhospitable ways of mysterious Tibet.

Explorer after explorer had tried to reach the capital at Lhassa, but no foreigner had actually made it to where the Dalai Lama sat. Perhaps Holmes, traveling under the alias of "a Norwegian named Sigerson," was there performing work for the Foreign Office, under the guidance of his brother Mycroft, the one individual in on the secret that Holmes had actually survived.

Some Sherlockians have speculated that these two years provided Holmes an opportunity to complete his Buddhist initiation and that he became a full-fledged Buddhist master. As we shall see in the next chapter, Holmes certainly carries about him the aura of a Zen teacher, a guru of awareness and observation. Perhaps this time of spiritual transformation explains why after his three-year hiatus, Holmes is never seen again using drugs to calm his teeming brain.

The man who passionately pursued so many secrets seems to have learned at last the Eastern wisdom found in the Tao: "Guard the senses, and life is ever full. . . . Seeing the small is insight." We will never know Holmes's true religious philosophy, but the Tao probably comes as close as we can guess when it states that secrets and their manifestations "being the same, they are called mysteries, mystery upon mystery—the gateway to manifold mysteries."

Whatever the truth (and Watson's clues are merely tantalizing, not conclusive), Holmes's interest in world religion is also shown during this time of freedom by including a dangerous trip through Persia, then a stop at Mecca, the holiest city to the faith of Islam, and a visit to the Caliph at Khartoum (where the English soldier Gordon had just been slaughtered, thus martyred to the cause of the British Empire—his portrait was the only other one to adorn the walls of 221-B, along with the American preacher Henry Ward Beecher's). A visit to Mecca, particularly at the time of the hajj, the great Moslem pilgrimage the prophet Mohammed had ordered all true believers to make at least once in their life, could have cost Holmes his life if he had been caught. No doubt this infidel's skill at disguise was here exercised to the fullest, but as we shall see, there are deeper disguises to come.

THE PARABLE IN THE PUZZLE

Leonard Holton's detective, the Roman Catholic priest Father Bredder, talks of being "a policeman of God." The priest sums up his ability to solve murders by saying, "I have to work from what I call spiritual fingerprints, which I find are just as useful in identifying people as physical fingerprints." One does not have to be religious to teach others how to begin reading the world, and the human heart, for the experience of mystery. We think of Sherlock Holmes as the archetypal detective, the sleuth supreme, and if we take at all seriously the idea of the spiritual seeker as a detective of the sacred, then it is not surprising that there are more religious undertones in the Doyle stories than we have ever noted before.

More than this, however, we love the stories of Sherlock Holmes because these tales are more than detective stories—they are humble parables for our instruction, the clarifying of our inner vision. We need stories to tell us "what other people don't know," narratives artfully contrived to gently and entertainingly answer the words of the Apocrypha (from Judith 8:16): "You cannot plumb the depths of the human heart nor find out what a man is thinking; how do you expect to search out God who made all things, and find out his mind or comprehend his thoughts?" Yet the omnipresent detective can plumb the heart of evil and read these spiritual fingerprints, so we wonder—can God's mystery be far behind?

The Hebrew word for the universe is *olam,* which comes from the word for "hidden." Yet the concept of mystery is less that which is unknown than that which is beyond human words and ideas. In other words, *mystery,* from the Greek word *mysterion,* is not about what we can solve but about what astonishes us in splendor and horror: that part of creation that can be experienced but never completely explained. This spiritual understanding of *mystery* is quite different from our common, everyday understanding of the term. *Mysterion* is about experiencing mystery as awe, not just as something secret and hidden.

Detective stories speak to the child in each of us, to the primal need to face the unknown and experience the terror and the exhilaration before this mystery. It is in childhood that most of us first encounter Sherlock Holmes, and I well

remember my own excitement in being given a large illustrated children's version at the age of nine by my mother. At
a five-and-dime on Main Street in Lexington, Kentucky, I
stood, mesmerized, looking at the colored pictures of a
snake curling down a bedpost; the glowing black fury of the
hound bounding for the throat of a prostrate figure; and
Holmes's fierce and intelligent face lit by the yellow glow of
his lantern. I remembered that gift, that first image of
Holmes, while driving down that same street several years
ago on the way to the Lexington Cemetery to bury her.

Yes, the mysteries of our life are staggering, and nothing
any detective writer has ever composed can touch the mystery of your own life, your story. Yet recalling my first
encounter with Holmes as he solves the story of "The
Speckled Band" in that child's version can still make my
skin crawl. It was there, in this comparably mild and safe
place, that I became acquainted not only with the frightening (and yet alluring) knowledge that evil exists and is real,
but also with the equally powerful hope that a power exists
to subdue, to triumph over such darkness. Such is the detective.

Holmes shouts as the villain of "The Speckled Band" dies
by his own murderous method: "It is a swamp adder! the
deadliest snake in India. He has died within ten seconds of
being bitten. Violence does, in truth, recoil upon the violent,
and the schemer falls into the pit which he digs for another."
This is strong stuff, and shows that the mystery story can
do far more than merely entertain us. It can educate us
about the nature of reality, in its evil and its beauty.

In Holmes's dramatic shout about the schemer falling
into the pit, we should recognize more than just his excitement. He is in fact making a rather sophisticated reference

to Ecclesiastes 10:8: "He that diggeth a pit shall fall into it; and whoso breaketh an hedge, a serpent shall bite him." In this case, of course, this is no metaphor—the serpent is quite real, and so is the rebounding violence. This is the kind of biblical quotation that cuts very deep indeed.

This kind of education comes to us in almost every Holmes tale, and, in fact, mystery stories are not puzzles so much as a kind of fairy tale mixed with religious ritual. The novelist Reynolds Price recalls: "All my childhood stories, I see now, were mysteries. I heard them as mysteries, whatever they were. What they were at first was Bible stories. . . . I had signed on for life as a sort of detective by the time I was four." He goes on to wonder: "*Why are they doing this?* Abraham to Isaac? Jesus to Mary? my father and mother to their lovely selves. . . . What I remember is the whole wider bafflement. The world was all a puzzle, just the little world around me; and that was growing daily."

It does not matter how old we grow, or how much our world expands—we still need stories to guide us. We cannot solve life's mystery, but we can become more and more aware of how we live *within* the mystery, and how the mystery dwells within us, not merely beyond and outside of ourselves. As Holmes tells his friend, "Education never ends, Watson. It is a series of lessons with the greatest for last."

Holy Clues is a book that finds parables where others have not noticed them before—though I suspect all lovers of mystery stories have been quietly affected and shaped by the spiritual fingerprints found within these entertainments. We will encounter many clues that the spiritual searcher must follow to find the sacred secrets within, *and this is particularly true for those of us with a modern, sci-*

entific, skeptical attitude. If you've already been given all the answers and know all mysteries, this book will not charm you. But if you have not, let us then follow the intriguing clues of guilt, goodness, evil, and the very texture of this world, to trace the spiritual fingerprints left behind by a mysterious God. Let us, for a time, put ourselves in the hands, as does Watson, of the master:

"What can you gather from this battered old felt?" Watson asks, in "The Blue Carbuncle."

"Here is my lens. You know my methods."

"I can see nothing."

"On the contrary, Watson, you can see everything."

1 * The Master's Instructions

THE WORST ROOMMATE of all time must have been Mr. Sherlock Holmes, who kept tobacco in the toe of his slipper, performed malodorous chemical experiments at all hours, saluted his queen by forming the letters *V.R.* on his Baker Street walls with bullet holes, and, in general, lived a chaotic and eccentric life.

The worst part of all for the faithful John H. Watson, fiction's most famous roomie, must have been the many and wearying demonstrations of his own slowness in the mental department. Dr. John H. Watson is not a fool, but he accepts that part of the bargain of being Holmes's partner in adventure is to have to endure being shown up over and over: "I trust that I am not more dense than my neighbors, but I was always oppressed with a sense of my own stupidity in my dealings with Sherlock Holmes." In fact, it is an old narrative trick, as old as the easily awed questioners of Socrates and the inability of Jesus' disciples to understand the message of their teacher, highlighting genius with an ordinary soul standing in for you and me. Besides, Holmes cannot be a teacher without a dutiful student.

At the beginning of the first short story, "A Scandal in Bohemia," Holmes performs his favorite trick, one that often begins the stories. He deduces from small details of Watson's appearance, clothing, and shoes that his friend has been walking in the country, has a careless servant girl, and is back in medical practice. After carefully detailing how he picked up all the little clues, Watson laughs. "When I hear you give your reasons, the thing always appears to me to be so ridiculously simple that I could easily do it myself, though at each successive instance of your reasoning I am baffled until you explain your process. And yet I believe my eyes are as good as yours."

Holmes agrees, and makes one of the most important statements in all the canon: "You see, but you do not observe."

Then he challenges Watson to state how many steps lead to 221-B, steps he has climbed hundreds of times.

"How many? I don't know."

"Quite so! You have not observed. And yet you have seen. That is just my point."

The answer is seventeen, a relatively insignificant fact, to be sure, but Holmes is absolutely insistent that each one of us must learn to see this world in just such a clear way. Watson never quite awakens to the fact that he is living with someone as focused as a Zen master, a spiritual teacher who just happens to have a fondness for tracking down criminals. Despite the light tone of the stories and their sly wit, Holmes is not playing a game with his "teachings" but rather enacting quite serious demonstrations about how to truly see our world. These stories are, at last, not just about apprehending criminals, but about apprehending reality. The detective is instructing his friend to learn what Buddhists call "bare attention." An old Zen tale describes a student badgering the teacher Ichu over and over about the core of the teaching. The master writes with his brush the word *Attention*. Not satisfied, the student asks, "Is that it?" In response, he writes, *Attention, Attention*. Now irritated, the student replies, "What is profound about that?" Writing the word three times, he calmly answers, "Attention means attention."

Which means the moment of perception before our thoughts take over, before our concepts and notions intervene. Bare attention is seeing things as they exactly are. Holmes sees with brilliance, true, but he sees, more importantly, with keen accuracy and without grand theories that twist truth into ideas and down blind alleys. The Buddhist psychotherapist Mark Epstein describes bare attention as "impartial, open, nonjudgmental, interested, patient, fearless, and impersonal."

Jesus speaks to this in Matthew, alluding to Isaiah's observation that "You shall indeed hear but never understand, and you shall indeed see but never perceive. . . ." To which Jesus adds: "Blessed are your eyes, for they see, and your ears, for they hear. Truly, I say to you, many prophets and righteous men longed to see what you see, and did not see it . . ." (13:16). Not to mention police!

You and I are generally used to seeing things the way Watson does. Holmes is not content, however; he clearly thinks *anyone* can reach insight in the way we approach seeing. The problem is that our usual vision is equivalent to blindness. The Jewish writer Abraham Joshua Heschel states it in another fashion: "The demand, as understood in Biblical religion, is to be alert and open to what is happening. . . . Every moment is a new arrival, a new bestowal." Perhaps the worst sin, then, is to stop paying attention.

This chapter is perhaps the very heart of this book, outlining five principles drawn from the Holmes stories that show us how to see with new attention. I caution you, however, not to make the mistake of thinking that simply *seeing with our eyes* is the point. It is said Helen Keller was once asked if there was anything worse than being blind. She replied, "Having no vision."

An intriguing illustration of this is to be found in the Max Carrados detective stories that appeared in the *Strand* magazine, an attempt to capitalize on the popularity of the Holmes tales and which, unlike the vast majority of Sherlock's rivals, are actually still readable. (There is nothing as effective for raising your opinion of Arthur Conan Doyle as a writer than to read the dated and painfully dull works written in imitation of him.) The twist is that Max Carrados is blind. In the introductory story, "The Coin of Dionysus," Max tells his friend Carlyle, "Do you know, Louis, I always had a secret ambition to be a detective myself. . . . That makes you smile?"

"Well, certainly, the idea—"

"Yes, the idea of a blind detective—the blind tracking the alert—" Max replies.

But in fact, it is Carrados who solves the mysteries, not his sighted friend. Ernest Bramah wrote of his blind detective that he is "blind, quite blind, but so far from crippling his interests in life or his energies, his blindness has merely impelled him to develop those senses which in most of us lie half dormant and practically unused." It is unlikely that any of us will ever uncover a murderer, but no mystery in our lives can ever be solved without insight and, as we shall see, a little artistic vision. What is dormant within us must be brought to life, made vivid.

These following five instructions from the Master are what we need to become people capable of such inner vision and insight.

(1) NOTHING IS LITTLE

When Watson first meets the young Holmes in the short novel *A Study in Scarlet,* Holmes is just embarking on his new career as a consulting detective in the great city of London. He quickly establishes himself as essential to the police, as well as to all classes of people, from common folk to royalty, because he notices things other people miss. At the scene of a murder, Holmes spends more time there than anyone else, picking up small physical clues after the police have already thoroughly searched the premises. Watson, just getting to know Holmes, finds he resembles nothing so much as a "pure-blooded, well-trained foxhound" as he paces the bloody scene, measuring between marks "quite invisible to me," gathering up a small pile of gray dust, and then examining with his magnifying glass the word *Rache* scrawled on the wall in red.

"They say that genius is an infinite capacity for taking pains," he tells Watson. "It's a very bad definition, but it does apply to detective work."

And what are these pains? As Holmes explains to Gregson, the befuddled policeman, "To a great mind, nothing is little."

Watson once complimented him for "having an extraordinary genius for minutiae." The detective replies simply that he appreciates their importance, and goes on to talk of taking impressions of footsteps and studying the distinguishing marks of various professions "with lithotypes of the hands of slaters, sailors, cork-cutters, compositors, weavers and diamond-polishers." And again, in another case, Holmes remarks, "It has long been an axiom of mine that the little things are infinitely the most important."

Over and over, the path to truth is to be found in the crevices of the floor, the cracks in the wall, in the disturbed dust. In looking for the big picture, we usually miss the very texture of reality that is ours to know. The poet William Blake is right that

> To see the World in a Grain of Sand,
> And a Heaven in a Wild Flower,
> Hold Infinity in the palm of your hand
> And Eternity in an hour

is the way to see all. True religion, like the pursuit of truth in mysteries, is the realization that everything that happens is crucial, that what happens in the details of the weave of chance and fate is not just important, but absolutely and extraordinarily important: lit by a searchlight, illuminated in meaning.

The little things are the signals to what is ultimately crucial. If detective fiction has any importance beyond entertainment, it is in the lesson that meaning is found in kneeling down to the small, the overlooked, the pieces and shards of our days. I once heard John Updike say, "Eternity is littleness piled high." It takes genius to see that low.

For all the emphasis Holmes places on reason and fact, there is a hidden mystical side to the Great Detective. Waiting to capture the Treasure of Agra in a stirring boat chase upon the Thames in *The Sign of Four*, Holmes points out the beauty of the scene spread before them. "How sweet the morning air is! See how that one little cloud floats like a pink feather from some gigantic flamingo. Now the red rim of the sun pushes itself over the London cloud-bank. It shines on a good many folk, but on none, I dare bet, who are on a stranger errand than you and I. How small we feel with our petty ambitions and strivings in the presence of the great elemental forces of Nature! ... The chief proof of man's real greatness lies in his perception of his own small-ness." It is in properly understanding what Holmes calls "a power of comparison and of appreciation" that we can break through to insight. Our chance for greatness lies in training our vision to see what we usually overlook.

In the aftermath of leaving behind the Roman Catholi-cism of his youth, young Dr. Doyle filled many notebooks with ruminations similar to those he later put in the mouth of Holmes. He wrote: "A religion to be true must include everything from the amoeba to the milky way." Nothing must be excluded from our view and purview for any faith to be true.

Everything rests on the small. Every detective knows the case opens at the point of the overlooked bent blade of grass, the ripped laundry stub, the hair, the fiber, the bestirred grime. What is astonishing is that Doyle invented this method, this way of seeing reality, even before he imagined Holmes. Also scrawled in these early notebooks is the nota-tion: "The coat-sleeve, the trouser-knee, the callosities of the forefinger and thumb, the boot—any one of these might tell us, but that all united should fail to enlighten the trained observation is incredible." So he proceeded to invent a char-acter who could notice exactly these things.

G. K. Chesterton once jokingly alluded to this attribute of mystery tales featuring "hawk-like amateur detectives" (read: Sherlock): "The latter finds near the corpse a boot-lace, a button hook, a French newspaper, and a return ticket from the Hebrides; and so, relentlessly, link by link, brings the crime home to the Archbishop of Canterbury."

He said of the Holmes stories that they were "perfectly

graceful and conscientious works of art." What made them great was the ironic notion of a powerful intellect like Holmes obsessed with the "small things" instead of the great: "it constitutes a kind of wild poetry of the commonplace."

That is exactly what the parables of detective fiction give us, over and over. "Every stone or flower is a hieroglyphic of which we have lost the key," added Chesterton, who understood so well the strange kind of wisdom found in these entertainments. We love detectives because we trust them to reveal that the world contains truth, not chaos; clues, not dead ends. And, above all, that it will be the "small things" that will take us there, not grand abstractions.

Our muddled and muddy lives have structure and order, and the detective reveals it to us when it has been obscured by lies and violence. Jacques Barzun, perhaps the greatest critic of mystery fiction, says, "What happens in modern detective fiction is that objects . . . are taken literally and seriously. They are scanned for what they imply, studied as signs of past action and dark purposes. . . . Bits of matter matter."

Nothing is little, not even the mustard seed in Jesus' parable—so small you can hardly see it, and yet within it is something towering and great, the largest tree in the desert. As Jesus said in introducing this "wild poetry" of the small and the great and the true, "For there is nothing hid, except to be made manifest; nor is anything secret, except to come to light" (Mark 4:22). But for that to happen, the next step of realization must be taken.

(2) NOTICE WHAT YOU SEE

The first step in spiritual perception, which is, as Holmes says, that "the little things are infinitely the most important," must be followed by something equally important. When Watson praises Holmes, "You see everything," the detective resists, insisting that this skill is nothing special. Anyone can do it.

"I see no more than you, but I have trained myself to notice what I see," is his reply. When Watson further remarks that Holmes's deductions about a certain client, a woman, came from details "quite invisible," this will not stand.

"Not invisible but unnoticed, Watson. You did not know where to look, and so you missed all that was important."

Once we accept that the little things are crucial, we still have to "notice" what we are seeing. The world stands before us all in perfect clarity; it is our lenses of attention that are clouded and obscured. We do not have to train with Holmes to learn "the importance of sleeves, the suggestiveness of thumb-nails, or the great issues that may hang from a boot-lace," but we can learn how to observe what we see. There is an old Hassidic story about a rabbinical student who travels a great distance to visit a famous teacher, not in order to listen to his learned discourses but to see how he tied his shoelaces.

Some years ago, I interviewed the novelist Dan Wakefield about his spiritual autobiography *Returning,* and he told me about going to a Roman Catholic nun for spiritual direction, hoping she would have special "clandestine" prayer formulas that would provide him a direct link to God. Instead she told him to go look at a tree.

Unsure if a Unitarian was ready for even such a surprisingly simple assignment, Wakefield went out to the Boston Common and was overwhelmed by the tree he gazed at. "The tree was too big and complicated and intricate to begin to comprehend. Instead, I picked out something to look at that seemed more suited to my own powers of understanding: a blade of grass." Twenty minutes a day for two weeks he looked, and was amazed at the freshness of what he saw, "the aliveness of it." And his spiritual journey opened up from there. He was training himself to notice. There is a wonderful drawing of Holmes by illustrator Sidney Paget showing the long form of the detective sprawled on the ground, carefully absorbed in studying the grass.

I was reminded of Dan's experience when I was preparing a class on "Buddhism in America" and discovered this quote from Van Gogh in a letter from Arles that described the effect Japanese woodblock prints was having on him: "We see a man who is undoubtedly wise, philosophic and intelligent who spends his time doing what? In studying the distance between the earth and the moon? No. In studying Bismarck's policy? No. He studies a blade of grass."

Did not Jesus demand of his disciples over and over—

"Let those who have eyes, let them see; let those who have ears, let them hear"?

This is a hard and lengthy lesson to learn. Too often, religion for us is great abstractions, big ideas, verbose theologies. Simple awareness? Why bother, when we can float on clouds of metaphysical notions?

Noticing what you see means you are present and accounted for in your own life. Spinning great theories is not the detective's task, nor is it ours. A little bare attention goes a long way. Chesterton, who knew his way around a mystery story, said that a detective story was the only form of literature that actually conveyed "some sense of the poetry of everyday life," because it presented our life back to us, each stone, brick, and signpost a hieroglyphic.

Some time ago, after presenting the ideas in this chapter to a men's group I belong to, a member who was an eye doctor came up to me. "What kind of doctor was Arthur Conan Doyle?" he asked. I answered, with a little bit of bluff, that I believed he was a general practitioner. Later, I had to go back to my questioner with a more precise answer. Holmes's creator, when he started writing the popular short stories, had actually just opened up a new office in London's Harley Street. Doyle had recently retrained himself to be an ophthalmologist, an eye doctor! And when patients did not show up in his waiting rooms, Doyle's "part-time" writings revealed another way an eye specialist could help us to see.

The mystery in P. D. James's *A Taste for Death* is resolved by the finding of a simple button in an offering box—*but first you have to see a button.*

This is rarer than we can imagine. When we are grasping for truth, for insight, a button is the easiest thing in the world to miss.

The other problem with noticing what you see is that it takes time. Holmes shows us the benefits of taking one's time to see, really see. The detective must take time to let the eye adjust, to take in detail, to not let the sweep of the eye take away what is there for us to view. The artist Georgia O'Keeffe remarked, "Nobody sees a flower—really—it is so small it takes time—we haven't time—and to see takes time, like to have a friend takes time."

We are sleepwalkers, really. I once heard the story of the young priest starting out as a hospital chaplain and going through his first stack of admission cards. One read: "Does not want to see a priest unless she is unconscious." That is usually the way we want to take in truth!

The first time in my life I think I truly noticed what I saw was when I was twelve and a counselor at a YMCA camp along the Kentucky River. We took twenty young campers out past their bedtime, foregoing our nightly ghost story, to gaze at the night sky. We sat at the edge of a field overlooking the black river, facing a steep cliff face that towered over the far bank. I showed them the stars in their constellations, the Archer, the Crab, the Big and Little Dipper. The longer we stared upward, the more stars we could see, so far from any city whose light could drain away the array of summer stars flung above.

Across the quiet rush of the river, against the dark cliff, thousands of fireflies were sparking their pale green-yellow light, dotting the dark in random, shifting patterns. And I did not know what was more wondrous, the cold blue flickering stars above or the dancing glow of the fireflies. The children fell silent. For a moment, I was lost and yet more fully at home than I had ever felt before, truly seeing what my eyes beheld. There was no clear message, or moral imperative, or evocation of God's majesty. No, it was smaller than that, something not exactly mystical, but fully attentive, and receptive. My sight and my vision were aligned—one.

I often tell my congregation that they should not expect to "get" religion by attending church. But the process of worship should prepare and open them up to remember when they were touched by the divine, the moments in which they felt most alive. I believe this. But before we remember, we must first see. Perhaps the greatest mystery we ever confront is the visible, not the invisible.

Remember the conversation we began this segment with: Holmes and Watson trying to "read" the life details of a lady client? Holmes challenges his friend to recall exactly what she looked like.

Watson begins, with the confidence of a well-trained physician, who, like a detective, has to read every day the at times subtle and hidden symptoms of illness. "Well, she had a slate-colored, broad-brimmed straw hat, with a feather of a brickish red . . ." the doctor begins, and goes on to describe her jacket, her dress, her gloves. "She had small round, hanging gold earrings, and a general air of being fairly well-to-do in a vulgar, comfortable, easy-going way."

Holmes applauds, chuckling. "You are coming along wonderfully. You have really done very well indeed. It is true that you have missed everything of importance, but you have hit upon the method, and you have a quick eye for color." Holmes delights in this friendly condescension, but then adds the real point: "Never trust to general impressions, my boy, but concentrate yourself upon details."

We so often miss everything of importance. In writing of his youth, Dostoevsky wrote: "In every tree, in every blade of grass that same mystery lies hid." Now we come to the third step of our progression, once we have learned to notice exactly what we see.

(3) THE DECEPTIVENESS OF THE ORDINARY

The bane of the brilliant deductor is that once you have painstakingly explained what your noticing of small details has lead you to, it no longer appears quite so magical. The comical "red-headed" character Jabez Wilson tells Holmes after a typically dazzling performance of reason and deduction, "I thought at first that you had done something clever, but I see that there was nothing in it, after all."

Ruefully, Holmes turns to his friend. "I begin to think, Watson, that I make a mistake in explaining." The detective, like the magician, knows that explanation can quickly deflate the sense of the miraculous, the marvelous. Not even Watson is immune to this.

In *The Hound of the Baskervilles*, after his friend has deduced that he has been in his club all day, and after hearing the reasoning explained to him, Watson bursts out, "Well, it is rather obvious."

Holmes replies, "The world is full of obvious things which nobody by any chance ever observes."

This response by Holmes is one of the wisest observations he ever makes. In fact, it is precisely the obvious, the fully commonplace and ordinary, that fools us again and again. Why is this? Perhaps because it is a function of our lenses of perception, the familiar is easily, and so quickly, lost to us. In the world of the intimately familiar, we so readily lose sight of what is important.

We lose sight even of what is holy. Every counselor has heard the bewildered cry of people grieving a loved one:

"And I can't even remember her face clearly," or, "I've forgotten his voice." The most elegant disguise for the sacred is right in plain sight. The ordinary is richly concealing because our eyes, our touch, our hearts are seduced to dullness. The grime of familiarity hides many a mystery. We think we have our world in view, but sometimes what is most crucial lies hidden in plain sight. In the Zen collection *The Gateless Gate,* it is put quite plainly: "It is too clear and so it is hard to see. A dunce once searched for a fire with a lighted lantern." And so it is. We search for truth with the answers inside us, we grasp for love with affection all around us, we long for treasures with riches heaped about us.

Mystery writers have known for a long time that the best place to hide a clue is right in plain sight, where we don't expect it. They have taken to heart the line in Congreve's play *The Double Dealer* that there is "No mask like open truth to cover lies, as to go naked is the best disguise."

In fact, one of the very first detective stories ever written, Edgar Allan Poe's "The Purloined Letter," has its solution in the missing letter being in the most glaringly obvious place—even as the police ransack everywhere it "should" be hidden.

We are so used to thinking of religious revelation coming into the world by thunder and lightning, miracles, and blinding visions that we too easily forget that spiritual truth is right here, right before us. It is just too obvious for us to notice.

Holmes teaches us the important lesson when he observes that "there is nothing so unnatural as the commonplace."

It is in the ordinary that the holy dwells, and it is not so much hiding as it is constantly being overlooked and neglected. We can get numbed, oblivious, to the spiritual reality contained within the everyday texture of life and relationships. There is an old story from the Eastern tradition that says that when the gods created the universe, they found a place for everything but the truth, and this created a problem, because the gods did not want this wisdom discovered right away. One of the gods suggested the top of the highest mountain, another the farthest star, a third spoke up for the dark side of the moon, and another for the bottom of the deepest ocean. Finally, they decided to place truth inside the human heart. In that way, we would search for it all over the universe, with the secret within us all the time.

It takes a rare observer to stay sharp, to keep the channels open—not for the mysterious, but for the ordinary. Sarah Coakley, a professor at the Harvard Divinity School, tells of hearing the frustration in the voice of a Russian scientist, a recent immigrant who was driving a taxi to make ends meet. In their new country, he feared, his children were losing "the capacity to attend."

Our culture "doesn't know the meaning of listening," the cabbie exclaimed, "it doesn't know how to focus—on a sound, on an idea, on each other, on God." Coakley thought as she listened to this expatriate's anguish she could hear the continuing refrain found in the Russian Orthodox liturgy of Saint John Chrysostom: "Wisdom, attend." This is what we are always being asked to do, and yet we so easily lose this attending, this holy curiosity for the surface of the life we have been presented. Heschel said simply that prayer is taking notice of the wonder of this world.

Deep into this book, I learned that the Church's main use of the word *mystery* is in regard to its sacraments: in Greek, the word is *mysterion*. Hearing Holmes talk about the world being "full of obvious things" nobody ever notices showed me just why sacraments can be called mysteries. Nothing is so ordinary as bread and wine, yet in the sacrament of communion these plain and unadorned materials are revealed as the very means of grace. Through the ordinary, what is unseen is now revealed. The Christian understanding of mystery is not what is hidden, but rather that *what is right there in plain sight is splendor once we are ready to attend.* The mystery is laced and threaded through every particle of *this creation*, the very physical and real foundation of all. It is like Jesus' parable of the yeast hidden in the dough, seeded in bread and ready to be revealed.

And if this is true, then there is a corollary to this third lesson. It is introduced in this way, as Holmes says to Watson in the story with which this section began, "The Red-Headed League": ". . . that for strange effects and extraordinary combinations we must go to life itself, which is always far more daring than any effort of the imagination."

"A proposition which I took the liberty of doubting."

"You did, Doctor, but none the less you must come round to my view, for otherwise I shall keep on piling fact upon fact on you until your reason breaks down under them and acknowledges me to be right."

Which leads us to step number four.

(4) THE BIZARRE IS NOT NECESSARILY MYSTERIOUS

At the beginning of "A Case of Identity," Holmes and Watson are sitting before a cozy fire in their Baker Street rooms.

"My dear fellow, life is infinitely stranger than anything which the mind of man could invent," Holmes ruminates. "We would not dare to conceive the things which are really mere commonplaces of existence."

He then proceeds to spin out a stunning vision worthy of J. M. Barrie, Doyle's friend who wrote the children's classic *Peter Pan*: "If we could fly out of that window hand in hand, hover over this great city, gently remove the roofs, and peep in at the queer things which are going on, the strange coincidences, the plannings, the cross purposes, the wonderful chain of events, working through generations, and leading to the most outré results, it would make all fiction with its conventionalities and foreseen conclusions most stale and unprofitable."

Anyone who works closely with people knows Holmes is right. The more you see, the more improbable and strange daily life appears. I sometimes consider writing about certain things I experience in my congregation, but my writerly instincts warn me: "No, that's too unlikely for any reader of fiction to accept." Real life has the continuing capacity to break free far beyond the constraints that a reader of fiction will ever accept!

And the great irony is this—that although the ordinary contains the most powerful of mysteries, Holmes also tells us to beware the allure of the bizarre. When Holmes is drawn into a murder investigation far from London, in the Boscombe Valley, he says, as he surveys newspaper accounts, "It seems, from what I gather, to be one of those simple cases which are so extremely difficult."

Watson, quite understandably, replies, "That sounds a little paradoxical."

"But it is profoundly true. Singularity is almost invariably a clue. The more featureless and commonplace a crime is, the more difficult it is to bring it home." He later says in the stories that the more bizarre a case appears, the less truly mysterious it actually is. Featureless crimes, on the other hand, could be totally baffling. In other words, the odder and more strange a matter, the greater will be the odds that the solution will be clear and straightforward.

I have often wanted to have inscribed across the portals of every church and temple this dictum of Holmes's: "It is a mistake to confound strangeness with mystery." This is a mistake people attracted to all forms of religious life can, and do, make.

In spirituality, we are often attracted by the grotesque, the outlandish, the startling and strange. We confuse these qualities with effusions of the divine. But the truth is that great spiritual masters urge their followers to beware the strange; that true enlightenment means a deeper appreciation of the very life in which we find ourselves. If we want mystery, it is never far from our sight: "What is mystery?" asked Dostoevsky. "Everything is mystery; in all is God's mystery. . . . Whether the tiny bird of the air is singing, or the stars in all their multitudes shine at night in heaven, the mystery is one, ever the same."

Beware the bizarre—it is too easily solved to be truly mysterious. I will further explore this attribute of faith in chapter five, but there is one thing I have learned to count on. You have to learn to be aware of, even to beware, the glittering power of the bizarre to divert our attention, our attending.

Concludes the Master: "For strange effects and extraordinary combinations we must go to life itself, which is always far more daring than any effort of the imagination."

Holmes is right. The mystery of the spiritual is not that of the fantastic, but of the simple.

The Tibetan teacher Chögyam Trungpa sounds a little like a detective when he concludes, "When you see ordinary situations with extraordinary insight it is like discovering a jewel in rubbish." The jewel was there all the time. The ordinary is blinding, and it takes time and patience to see the shining there when we are lulled and beguiled by the daily, the "mundane."

(5) PRESUME NOTHING

Over and over, Holmes restrains himself from jumping ahead of his perceptions. It is only natural, after absorbing the preceding four steps, to be ready to leap to conclusions. But wait. Wait some more.

In *The Hound of the Baskervilles* he states, "I presume nothing." He keeps his mind free, his options open. Bare attention is something very hard to accomplish. The first and last thing we bring to this way of seeing is a mind without theories, without preconceptions, without prejudices.

Bringing to our life a mind choked with judgments is, according to Holmes, a bad habit, but one we are prone to, because "human nature is weak." The problem is that some of our leaps of faith and leaps into faith can land us in disaster. But to face reality with an open mind and an attentive heart is a way of easing, not leaping, into faith.

"I make a point of never having any prejudices, and of following docilely wherever fact may lead me," claims the detective. There is no special spiritual virtue in believing ideas born of exclusion, paranoia, or cosmic insecurity. True faith isn't believing outlandish things, but being perfectly open and free to see the sacred in the ordinary and the commonplace. There is a Zen saying that Holmes would surely have approved of: "If your mind is empty, it is always ready for anything—it is open to everything."

For some years I was mystified by an enigmatic comment the great detective makes in "The Noble Bachelor": "Circumstantial evidence is occasionally very convincing, as when you find a trout in the milk, to quote Thoreau's example." It was not much clearer when I finally found Thoreau's words, a journal notation dated November 11, 1850. Still, it has a certain jaunty charm about it. A great flapping trout in one's milk jug certainly is convincing that *something* is up!

It is odd to hear the urbanized Holmes quote someone seemingly as different from himself as the American nature-mystic Henry David Thoreau. Then I remembered a passage of Thoreau's from my denomination's hymnal: "I wish to live deliberately, to front only the essential facts of life. . . . We must learn to awaken and keep ourselves awake. . . ."

The notion of the thin, hawk-nosed naturalist gazing with absolute clarity on the minute and exquisite details of the natural scene around Concord is not far at all from our notion of Holmes stalking through his yellow-fogged London. It was Thoreau who counseled patience in seeing what is before us. "Nature will bear the closest inspection. She invites us to lay our eye level with her smallest leaf, and take an insect view of its plain."

He even fancied himself a form of detective: "I long ago lost a hound, a bay horse, and a turtledove, and am still on their trail." Above all, he seemed to be describing the perceptual genius of Holmes when he wrote: "The millions are awake enough for physical labor; but only one in a million is awake enough for effective intellectual exertion, only one in a hundred million to a poetic or divine life. To be awake is to be alive. I have never yet met a man who was quite awake."

Maybe this is why Doyle has Holmes quote Thoreau. Holmes is trying to teach Watson, and us, how to awaken our senses, how to move past sight into insight and then into a Zen-like state of realization fused to fact. When you think about it, the naturalist could well have been a model for Holmes. Emerson said of his friend, speaking as a Watson figure, "It was a pleasure and a privilege to walk with him. . . . One must submit abjectly to such a guide, and the reward was great. Under his arm he carried an old music book to press plants; in his pocket, his diary and pencil, a spy glass for birds, microscope, jack-knife and twine." In wonderment, Emerson concluded that his companion possessed a "power of observation that seemed to indicate additional senses. He saw as with a microscope, heard as with an ear trumpet, and his memory was a photographic register of all he saw and heard."

Thoreau's later journals reveal another incident that helps us be cautious when confronting evidence. On a January winter morning in 1860 the naturalist, on the tracks of a fox, comes upon bloody and tramped-down snow after a rabbit's tracks lead away from his companions. A bit of tail, some entrails, some fragments of slate-colored fur; nothing more is left of the rabbit. He looks at the lines of tracing in the snow and thinks a bird has taken up the rabbit until interrupted by a hungry fox. Then, like a detective, he follows the clues until he finds the frozen body. "I thought, Perhaps he has carried off to his young, or buried, the rest. But as it turned out, though the circumstantial evidence against the fox was strong, I was mistaken." Mistaken, because he subsequently spied the signs of an owl, the most likely other culprit during a fox's night hunting hours. Sherlock Holmes could not have done better, thirty years on! "The circumstantial evidence against the fox was very strong, for the deed was done since the snow fell and I saw no other tracks but his at the first places. Any jury would have convicted him, and he would have been hung, if he could have been caught." It was the owl who murdered, not the fox. It pays to look twice, and then wait some more.

On the other hand, to come at reality without prejudices or preordained views means, at times, that we can sense and experience something truly miraculous without rejecting it outright. And this approach to truth leads naturally to one of the Master's most famous sayings. Next to what the dog did in the nighttime (which was, surprisingly, nothing), the most well known part of the canon is Holmes's dictum: "How often have I said to you that when you have eliminated the impossible, whatever remains, *however improbable*, must be the truth?"

To gaze at the world with bare attention and an open curiosity can lead us to improbable places and unlikely solutions to the holy. When we learn to presume nothing, we can see everything, anything.

We may mostly live and see like Watson, but there are paths to observing like Holmes. He insists that anyone can learn to observe what we see. All it takes is a steadfast inner confidence in the method, and a willingness to face the unknown. Albert Einstein said, "It is enough if one tries merely to comprehend a little of this mystery every day. Never lose a holy curiosity."

But it is not scientists or detectives I think of here. I have found that the people who teach me to live with holy curiosity allied to this willingness to "presume nothing" are not spiritual writers at all, but artists. Indeed, the painter we have already quoted, Van Gogh, once wrote his brother that the path of the artist was that of someone who "has paid attention to the things he sees with his eyes and hears with his ears, and has thought them over; he will end in believing, and he will perhaps have learned more than he can tell. To try to understand the real significance of what the great artists, the serious masters, tell us in their masterpieces, *that* leads to God."

The passion aroused by the radical painters of Holmes's own time—the Impressionists and their successors—came from their rejection of a false realism. They painted how the eye actually perceives light, the way things look in the flux and movement of light. They rejected paintings that were precise, that were more about ideas and preconceptions of "truth" than about how our eyes actually perceive the world. These painters "presumed nothing" and painted accordingly. That is what made the Impressionists shocking. It is, as Holmes says, human nature to see what we expect to see, and that is why we so seldom observe and notice what we see.

You are probably thinking we are a long distance from Mr. Sherlock Holmes, yet Doyle has laid the clues cunningly for us. In "The Greek Interpreter," Watson is surprised to hear Holmes speak for the first time about his family roots. "In your own case," says Watson, "from all that you have told me it seems obvious that your faculty of observation and your peculiar faculty for deduction are due to your own systematic training."

Holmes answers that his ancestors were average country squires, "But, none the less, my turn that way is in my veins, and may have come with my grandmother, who was

the sister of Vernet, the French artist." (The reference is to a real person: Émile Jean Horace Vernet, who died in 1863.) Then Holmes states the revealing conclusion: "Art in the blood is liable to take the strangest forms."

Nothing could be odder than the artistic vision finding its employment in apprehending guilty thieves and murderers, but Holmes had it right—his skill is, in the end, more than reason and logic, but an artistic one. We see this at the very beginning of the stories, when in his first mystery Holmes thanks Watson, "I might not have gone but for you, and so, missed the finest study I ever come across: a study in scarlet, eh? Why shouldn't we use a little art jargon." There is, he notes, "the scarlet thread of murder running through the colorless skein of life, and our duty is to unravel it, and isolate it, and expose every inch of it."

The detective is presented as a special sort of artist all through his career; as Watson notes: "Holmes had the impersonal joy of the true artist in his better work"; and again, "Holmes, like all great artists, lived for his art's sake. . . ." Even Holmes laughs about himself: "Watson insists that I am the dramatist in real life. Some touch of the artist wells up in me. . . ."

This grandnephew of the painter Vernet expressed "the strangest forms" of the artistic vision, and he shows us again and again how to break out of the stale and stolid ways of seeing in preconceived ways. Step by step, he explains to Watson how to observe, how to reach the state of "bare attention." How to attend. How to value and treasure the smallest details of the world set before us. How to realize that at last nothing is little.

Many years ago I was working on a sermon while my son, who was four, played with miniature cars next to me with the serene concentration of the child. I idly asked him what love was. Without looking up, he said, "Love is the eyes we see with." I made a promise to my family a long time ago not to use them as sermon illustrations, but I will never forget the cold chill I got as I hurriedly scratched his definition down. I have never found a better way to express it.

Any faith is a way of seeing, an inner vision that can become true to reality and as vibrant as a Van Gogh painting with curling, swirling color that reveals the objects of the world bathed in light and reflecting and revealing their full energy and power. To see deeply and well *and accurately* is to know that nothing is invisible, but rather simply unseen.

The mark of a good spiritual teacher is that, no matter how demanding, how irritable, how pressing, how paradoxical and mystifying he or she might be, they ultimately never give up on us. Holmes never lets Watson believe for a moment that his eyes are not as good as his. Now it is time for us to observe what we see, alert and open to what is happening.

2 * The Case of the Missing God

HOLMES, LIKE MANY a sensitive, hyperacute soul, is extremely prone to periods of melancholy, especially when engrossing and suitably bizarre situations are not on hand to energize his consciousness. In "The Retired Colourman," the last published tale (though not the last one written), as Watson enters the Baker Street flat of his friend he passes a client leaving.

"Did you see him?" asks Holmes.

"You mean the old fellow who has just gone out?"

"Precisely."

"Yes, I met him at the door."

"What did you think of him?"

"A pathetic, futile, broken creature."

"Exactly, Watson. Pathetic and futile. But is not all life pathetic and futile? Is not his story a microcosm of the whole? We reach. We grasp. And what is left in our hands in the end? A shadow. Or worse than a shadow—misery."

These words, written by Doyle so near the end of the Holmesian canon, could be read as a final reflection on the stories themselves. These despairing words better describe Holmes's inner spiritual bleakness than the appearance of client Josiah Amberley (though Holmes, for all his claims of serene, logical distance from others, was actually quite empathetic and attuned to the pain and distress of those who sought him out). Yet these despairing philosophical words reveal that for all of Holmes's considerable wisdom and moral power, he just might be the last person for us to go to for godly insight or religious reassurance. The old image of the stuffy Victorian God reigning in Heaven with Queen Victoria below, presiding over an empire where "all's right with the world," does not apply here. Despite Holmes's gentlemanly appearance, he conceals a radical sensibility within. His is not a sunny, blissful spirituality.

That despairing passage reminds me of a story, probably apocryphal, of a friend of Samuel Beckett (author of bleak, existential plays such as *Waiting for Godot*). Greeting the playwright before embarking on a walk with him, the friend observed, "What a gorgeous day this is! Why, it makes you feel good to be alive!"

Beckett thought a moment, looking about at the beautiful day. "Well, I wouldn't go that far."

The spirituality of Sherlock Holmes is not one directed to a warm, loving Father God.

Our detective's suspicion that all our grasping efforts for enlightenment are doomed to nothing but shadows leads to a natural question: Is Holmes an atheist?

As we shall see, he is not; but his vision of God is somehow peculiarly applicable to the modern sensibility, in which God somehow seems missing in action, a void, a shadow, a presence evoked by the whiff of retreating incense. For so many people, even those still in the pews, the notion of the Kingly God who judges all and presides over the cosmos is becoming more and more problematic. Emily Dickinson described God as a recluse, writing: "I know that He exists / Somewhere—in—silence."

As a Unitarian minister, I minister every day to people who share some of Holmes's theological caution, which often verges on despair. It is said, only half-kiddingly, that my denomination begins all prayers with the invocation

"To Whom It May Concern . . ." The questions Unitarians ask about the shadowy God in their lives can be very painful indeed. Assurances of God's magnificence and power ring hollow to them. Their spiritual quest seems headed into a void. This "silent" God is in fact the one many people are in search of: the only God they now possess, if they have not altogether abandoned belief.

THERE BUT FOR THE GRACE OF GOD

Yet, for many, I suspect, this spiritual bleakness is exactly what makes Holmes all the more trustworthy as a spiritual guide. He seems to regard the idea of God with deep seriousness. God is not his best friend or his heavenly pal. God is not in his hip pocket, a mystery easily solved and thus resolved. Holmes is not pious or religious in any orthodox sense, but that simply serves to make him all the more interesting to spiritual seekers who "thirst for the Living God" but at the same time find classic images and idols of God somehow disappointing, unfulfilling, and too meager by half.

Sherlock Holmes often evokes the deity, sometimes simply as a common phrase of emphasis (equivalent to "Holy Moses," "Jumping Jehovah," "Jeezus!" and other religious ejaculations drained of all sacred meaning), but sometimes also in moments that offer something far more insightful. For a man who seems so much above all common pieties and religious rituals, Holmes sees enough pain and heartache in his line of work to sense that there is a presence hovering within that shadow. It is in those times of darkness and despair that he talks to God.

At the close of "The Boscombe Valley Mystery," Holmes has left his usual urban haunts to expose the truth behind a murder in the countryside. In the course of establishing the innocence of the chief suspect, the murdered man's son, he finds himself in sympathy with the actual murderer. Holmes has the killer sign a full confession but promises to use it only as a last resort if he cannot free the accused young man otherwise. Holmes observes, "Well, it is not for me to judge you. I pray that we may never be exposed to such a temptation."

As the shattered and gravely ill man leaves them, Holmes, in the wake of his act of mercy, turns to Watson. He then speaks from the depths of his desolate view of life, but also from this equally strong sense that the divine is inscrutable and yet real: "God help us!" said Holmes after a long silence. "Why does fate play such tricks with poor, helpless worms? I never hear of such a case as this that I do not think of Baxter's words, and say, 'There, but for the grace of God, goes Sherlock Holmes.' "

The fact that Holmes wrongly attributes the Protestant martyr John Bradford's words to the dissenting minister Richard Baxter (whose pulpit I preached from for a year as a ministerial student in Kidderminster, England) does not take away the genuine pathos of his plea. Holmes's essential pessimism is mixed with a deep understanding that only a thin edge of grace prevents him, and for that matter any of us, from tasting these ashes of despair.

This seeming nihilism is firmly set in the midst of mercy, of a refusal to judge or to stand superior to others, and all this happens under the shadow, the obscure shade, of God.

This kind of reference to God arises often in the stories, such as when he makes a nearly disastrously late deduction in "The Disappearance of Lady Frances Carfax" and cries, "Good heavens, Watson, what has become of any brains that God has given me?"; and again, when he vows in anguish, after failing to save the life of John Openshaw in "The Five Orange Pips," that he will track down the murderous conspirators: "It becomes a personal issue with me now, and, if God sends me health, I shall set my hands on this gang."

Lastly, he invokes God when he describes to Watson how he survived yet another attack on him (after Professor Moriarty's failed attempt) on the slippery rocky chasm above the Reichenbach Falls. After hiding himself in a rock ledge to observe Watson's return, one of Moriarty's assistants who had also waited on the steep hill above began rolling down great rocks over Holmes, and he was forced to scramble down the deadly incline to escape with his life, or join the professor at the foot of the falls. "I don't think I could have done it in cold blood. It was a hundred times more difficult than getting up. But I had no time to think of the danger, for another stone sang past me as I hung by my hands from the edge of the ledge. Halfway down I slipped, but, by the grace of God, I landed, torn and bleeding, upon the path."

Holmes's "resurrection" at the Reichenbach Falls was a near-run thing, and even the skeptic Holmes had to invoke some greater power than his own as he so narrowly escaped oblivion.

Holmes is like most of us, summoning God's name when he is pressed to the edge, or cast down in desperation. Still, few would point to him as having a warm, cozy relationship with the Almighty, or see him as a religious exemplar. Holmes is not an atheist, but is close to it. God for him is a specter hovering on the edge of life's desperation, not a powerful presence or a comforter. In fact, the detective Ellery Queen sums up Holmes's whole attitude toward the divine when he observes in *The Lamp of God*: "No riddle is esoteric unless it's the riddle of God; and that's no riddle—it's a vast blankness."

For many of us, God has become not just the riddle in the middle of the greatest mystery of all, but much like the corpse at the start of a mystery story, a corpse that has mysteriously disappeared, as if it had never existed at all. Yet to those who look closely, signs are still scattered everywhere that point to this presence as having indeed been there—evocative and tantalizing clues to God's existence that defy our despair, our bewilderment. For me, this is an excellent metaphor for the missing God, except that I sometimes wonder—in the midst of all of our efforts to track down the missing One, the pursued may in fact be trailing just behind us, seeking us.

DEITY AND DETECTIVES

God is literally a murdered corpse in Woody Allen's story "Mr. Big," in which a gumshoe named Kaiser is hired by a Vassar philosophy major to find a missing person. It turns out she wants to find God.

When Kaiser asks her what God looks like, she admits she has never seen him.

"Oh, great. Then you don't know what he looks like? Or where to begin looking?"

"No. Not really. Although I suspect he's everywhere. In the air, in every flower, in you and I—and in this chair."

"Uh-huh," Kaiser thinks. "So she was a pantheist."

Following the twists and turns of the parody investigation, Kaiser later gets a call from the police. He is asked if he's still looking for God, the "Great Oneness, Creator of the Universe, First Cause of All Things?"

The detective nods, and is told somebody exactly answering that description has just showed up at the morgue. They conclude the divine murder was a professional job. In fact, the police conclude it was done by an existentialist. When Kaiser asks why, the sergeant answers, "Haphazard way it was done. Doesn't seem to be any system followed."

I encountered this comic parable and parody as a college student, and to my astonishment, years later I find strange and intriguing parallels in my religious reading.

In his book *The Disappearance of God* Richard Elliot Friedman makes a provocative and interesting argument about the mysterious way God seems to be a strong and living presence in the early Hebrew scriptures but then, as the author bluntly concludes, "God disappears in the Bible." From the intimate communications of Eden and Mt. Sinai, the deity appears less and less, and comes to speak not at all. He quotes Deuteronomy 31:17, where God tells Moses, "I shall hide my face from them. I shall see what their end will be." The truth of Friedman's argument is beyond the bounds of this book, but what fascinates me is how he frames his task: "You may choose to approach these mysteries as one would a detective story. The research of scholars does resemble detective work in a variety of ways—clues, deduction, false starts, breakthroughs, patience, unexpected twists—presumably because so much of life is, after all, a mystery. . . . Like a detective's work, its task is to look for an explanation for what appears mysterious. A scholar, like a detective, need not set out to prove or disprove anything but rather to look for that explanation—which is to say, to try to find the truth."

All this might seem odd for those of us who grew up with comforting platitudes and the assurance of a God in heaven and on earth. God dead (or at least lost): the greatest missing-person report in history? This propensity of theologians to see themselves as investigators is seemingly everywhere. Recently, reading *Gospel Truth*, a brilliant exploration into the modern quest for the historical Jesus, I found the journalist Russell Shorto describing a roomful of Jesus scholars with this pithy observation: "It is an ideal setting for detective work. . . . These are indeed detectives, and the person they are searching for, whom they believe has been hidden by two thousand years of myth, is Jesus of Nazareth." Pages later Shorto concludes, "We have a two-bit detective inside us who demands just the facts. And so we dig." So again, when we dig deeper, we wind up with an empty tomb, and facing the greatest locked-room mystery escape ever. Queen's "riddle of God" is not going to be an easy one to solve.

The book of Deuteronomy phrases it just as Sherlock Holmes experiences the divine: God now has a hidden face, but still waits to see what is to become of us. The missing God is found in acts of human justice, and in a sense that justice is real, a kind of moral gravity that grounds and sustains all reality. This justice is not a sentiment, or a naïve projection, or an idle wish of a romantic. It is Holmes's judgment that this foundational divine judgment is true, and he is no tender or dreamy theologian!

Many years ago, I did a spiritual retreat with Gerald May, author of many insightful books on spirituality and psychology, and before an entire day of silence, he invited us to meditate upon our images of God. The phrase "the prodigal God" kept coming to mind. I recalled how often I felt pain and loss and yearning toward God, feelings that the father in Jesus' "prodigal son" parable must have felt as he waited upon a loved one in exile.

Then I thought of the times we are all forced to wait in our lives, places where absence can be a time of gestation, of a kind of longing so intense and fruitful that these times can become in truth a powerful kind of intimacy. I thought of images such as wandering in the wilderness, of the waiting of parents for the growth of a child in the dark womb, of the frozen seed in the soil during winter, of sleep and dreams in the night, of the times in our lives we are forced to wait, and wait, and wait. These are spiritual experiences we cannot do without, nor should we want to. They prepare us, they hallow us, they heighten and guide us. Times of waiting, like the Saturday before the dawn of Easter (when you don't even know that Easter awaits you) can become the holiest experiences of our days, if we are willing to endure, to hold on, to trust when trust seems as lost as we are.

VEILS OF LIGHT

One hesitates to take spiritual reading recommendations from someone as religiously dour and unsettled as Sherlock Holmes, but Watson does, in only their second adventure. *The Sign of Four* records Holmes doing exactly that, not once, but twice. First, when rushing out to follow a clue, he says, "I am going out now. I have some few references to make. Let me recommend this book—one of the most remarkable ever penned. It is Winwood Reade's *Martyrdom of Man*. I shall be back in an hour." (Of course, good old Watson finds he can't concentrate on this philosophical tome, his mind wandering toward thoughts of their client Mary Morstan, whom he later will marry.) A few chapters later, gazing at a group of rough workers leaving their job, Holmes observes (to his friend) that each may have a spark of immortality in him. "You would not think it, to look at them. . . . A strange enigma is man!" says Holmes.

Watson helpfully adds, "Someone calls him a soul concealed in an animal."

To which Holmes responds with a second mention of the radical writer: "Winwood Reade is good upon the subject," he begins, arguing that human activity is predictable in the mass. As always, Holmes sees human beings from a scientific rather than a romantic vantage point. Speculations on "the soul" leave him cold, but he is willing to wonder if we humans are beings whose actions can be studied and predicted—say, like ants in a colony, or like his beloved bees in their teeming hives. Holmes is willing, as well, to take philosophy seriously, and even the awesome judgments of God in the realm of justice, but not the cloud-cuckoo religious imaginative constructions of divinity, no matter how well-intentioned, ancient, or revered.

This Victorian best-seller Holmes praises has faded into oblivion, but it was a shocking book in its time, very radical in its religious tone and air of philosophical despair. It is strange to find *any* religious book touted in the middle of a taut little mystery, so there must be a reason, and there is. The young Dr. Doyle, like his creation, was enthusiastic about Reade's book, which was, at the heart of it, a rejection of Victorian pieties toward a personal God. Doyle wrote in his private notebook, "Winwood Reade considers that the true tendency is more and more away from a personal God—a God of reflected human ideas—and towards an unthinkable, impersonal force. Let us concentrate our attention more on serving our poor-devil neighbor and improving our own hearts!" Reade's anti-Christian themes were indeed, as Watson phrases it, "daring speculations."

It took a great deal of courage for Doyle to place in the lips of his young detective such a radical clue to his evolving personal religious beliefs. We read right past these references today, but Doyle's contemporary readers could not escape the conclusion that this strange and intriguing character Holmes held some fairly shocking and unusual views about God. So let me be as forthright as Doyle was a hundred years ago. Perhaps Martin Buber was right when he suggested, shockingly, "The atheist staring from his attic window is often nearer to God than the believer caught up in his own false image of God."

There are no truer words in the scriptures than those of Isaiah 45:15—"Verily thou art a God that hidest thyself." If God disappears and does not make clear a meaning, or shout from the rooftops, or send us miraculous e-mail or messages in the sky—then maybe we ought to trust that perhaps there is a stern but necessary discipline here, a way of faith that we can learn and accept. This is not *doubt* so much as a rigorous spiritual path of trust. Our images of God can be so inadequate, so petty and mundane, that they severely limit our sense of wonder and worship. A sense of mystery may become a better path to worship than entertaining the old formulas of divinity, worn and tired.

Not even the word *God* matters very much. As Forrester Church reminds us, "God is not God's name." The Jews had it right by treating God's name as a sacred blank, a word that could not be said or written, a silence that preserved the holy.

For many people, whatever their religion or their lack of same, they think that by backing away from these traditional notions they have somehow lost God. Maybe in fact they have made the first crucial step in reconnecting with God, the God who is beyond images that are too small, too tribal, too close to "Mr. Big." Perhaps the theological reticence of Holmes is a path to something holy. This is taking God seriously; this is the start of cleansing the palette so that we can at last taste divinity.

The case of the disappearing God is more complex than it first appears. It appears that we have not "lost" God so much as we have awakened to the opportunities of this hidden presence. The ancient Egyptians addressed God as a glory that was a veil of light. We think of light as that which reveals—but God's light is so bright, so magnificent, that it can be a veil to our eyes.

In the Talmud, it is said that the Roman emperor Hadrian ordered Rabbi Joshua Ben Hananiah, "I want to see your God."

The rabbi calmly replied, "You cannot see Him." But Hadrian angrily demanded his request be followed. So the rabbi asked that they go outdoors, and he positioned the emperor to face the sun and gaze at it, then at its height and blazing in blinding glare.

"I cannot," said Hadrian, shielding his eyes.

"If you cannot even look at the sun, which is just one of God's attendants, how do you presume to be able to look at the divine presence?" answered the rabbi.

And in what ways do we move toward this veil of light? As Holmes says, "We reach. We grasp."

THE LIGHT OF TRUTH

We cannot parade Holmes as a great mystic, however. His openness to God is somehow tied to his profession. In the story "The Problem of Thor Bridge" he confesses as much when he reaches a point of insight. At the sudden solution of the perplexing murder, he cries, "With the help of the god of justice I will give you a case which will make England ring."

God to Holmes may be a shadow, but there is one clear aspect to this divine reality. It is truth, it is clarity, it is literally this "god of justice." Modern philosophers may wallow in relativistic ethics, and recent detective novelists may give us novels where there is no clear right or wrong, where the detective remains mired in doubt even at the close—but this is not Holmes's way.

In Graham Greene's *The Honorary Consul* a radical priest has mistakenly kidnapped the wrong man in an attempt to shake up a corrupt South American government. As the story unfolds, we learn more about Father Rivas's political faith, which, on the surface, is stronger than his religious faith and his priestly vows. He has to decide if he really will kill Charley Fortnum, the mistaken man, but an effective enough pawn in the new world of political terrorism. Can Father Rivas kill an innocent man? Or will his first faith rise up against the other? In a time of waiting, he is asked what book he is reading—a breviary?

"Only a detective story. An English detective story." When asked if it is a good one, Father Rivas explains it is hard to tell, that the translation is poor, and besides, he can always guess the ending. "Oh, there is a sort of comfort in reading a story where one knows what the end will be. The story of a dream world where justice is always done. There were no detective stories in the age of faith—an interesting point when you think of it. God used to be the only detective when people believed in Him. He was law. Like your Sherlock Holmes. It was He who pursued the wicked man for punishment and discovered all." But now they shared a world where moral chaos reigned, with electric shocks on political prisoner's genitals, the chopping of fingers, tortures of the mind and spirit. In this new world, the old, tidy, ordered world of the English detective, backed by a firm and unyielding heavenly justice, seems more a fantasy. Now people like Father Rivas have to navigate their way through an ethical nightmare. But it is wrong to say that the moral center and refined judgment of Holmes is a mere cozy dream of the past.

The master detective adds in "Thor Bridge": "Take my assurance that the clouds are lifting and that I have every hope that the light of truth is breaking through." In this case, Holmes has the formidable task of dealing with Mr. J. Neil Gibson, the Gold King, a powerful American financier who is used to having his way and letting money shove aside all obstacles to his gratification. Holmes, normally the gentleman, bristles instinctively at Gibson's aggressiveness. He even sternly lectures him, "Some of you rich men have to be taught that all the world cannot be bribed into condoning your offenses." He spars with him, prodding and pushing, to break him down. After exploding in anger, yet reluctant to admit less-than-noble intentions toward Miss Grace Dunbar, the family governess charged with the shooting of his wife Maria, Gibson finally and grudgingly concedes. "Well, the stakes are down and the reserve open, and you can explore where you will. What is it you want?"

Holmes answers, "The truth."

That is all Holmes ever wants. He refuses fame and fortune over and over in these tales, all because his focus is on *truth*—which he believes to have a powerful reality above all others. This "god of justice" is the only God Holmes can worship, and it is not an orthodox kind of devotion, to be sure, though it is compelling, sustaining, and utterly real to him.

When at the close of this case "the light of truth" has broken through, Holmes's somewhat dark theology is expressed again when he wonders if Mr. J. Neil Gibson has learned "something in that schoolroom of sorrow where our earthly lessons are taught." Holmes is not in the business of speculating about the lessons of a heavenly life, but earthly sorrow, he knows, can humble a man and break him down enough to learn at last what truths life has to offer us. Even a Gold King can be changed. The light of truth is strong, and even if all of our grasping for God leaves us only with a shadow, there is still one sure path to reality open to us. God is a god of justice, and to Holmes, that is no illusion, no idol. He has staked his life on that.

One early Church writer calls God's truth a "dazzling obscurity of the secret silence, outshining all brilliance with the intensity of their darkness." Even in God's shadow, there is the dazzling of truth. To trust in this power does not require any divine fireworks or spectacular miracles. It requires a heightened progression of our ability to discern truth, to judge others (and ourselves) wisely, and, as we shall discuss later in this book, to learn mercy.

While writing this section, something kept nagging at me. The story of Elijah presented itself, and if you want the whole tale, it is in 1 Kings 17–19. It seems Elijah, as prophets are wont to do, has shown up the king through faith in Yahweh—and King Ahab and his Baal-loving wife, Jezebel, respond by wanting him dead. He flees into the wilderness in a state of profound depression, actually asking God to kill him.

Finally Elijah hides in a cave, but after a time an inner voice tells him to stand on a nearby mount "before the Lord." Then follows one of the most powerful passages of world religion, a key turning point, I think, in human consciousness. A great wind comes and shatters the rock, but God is not there. Then comes an earthquake, but again, God is absent. Finally a fire rages, but in the memorable phrase, "the Lord was not in the fire; and after the fire a still small voice." Personally, I prefer the New Revised Standard translation of this revelation of God through conscience: "a sound of sheer silence."

God may arrive in silence, but it is a silence that is greater than all the special effects Hollywood has ever devised.

HE WHO IS GONE

In the cathedral at Canterbury in southeast England, there is a hallowed space near where Thomas à Becket was killed, murdered by King John's men. There is no mystery about who did the deed, or why.

But something *is* puzzling about T. S. Eliot's treatment of the event in his verse play *Murder in the Cathedral*. A "tempter" from the king has come to Becket and is offering the rebellious archbishop a deal: in return for recovering great personal political power and even the chancellorship, all Becket must do is submit his will to the king and not to the Church.

Becket faces the king's tempter, and asks these enigmatic questions:

> "Who shall have it?"
> The tempter replies, "He who will come."
> "What shall be the month?"
> "The last from the first."
> "What shall we give for it?"
> "Pretense of priestly power."

Some Sherlockians heard, when they read these lines, a certain haunting similarity. These questions had been asked before, somewhere. And turning to their trusty canon, sure enough, they found "The Musgrave Ritual," a very early case of Holmes's brought to him by an old university friend.

Reginald Musgrave describes to Holmes a bizarre family ritual that every male Musgrave has preserved for three hundred years, a memorized statement that no one seems to understand:

Whose is it?
His who is gone.
Who shall have it?
He who will come.
What was the month?
The sixth from the first.
What shall we give for it?
All that is ours.

T. S. Eliot has clearly taken Becket's (and the tempter's) words from this Doyle detective story, but why? Why does Eliot choose in this play to follow his own whimsical observation about writing: "Immature poets imitate; mature poets steal."

Holmes uses his skills and insight to eventually solve the puzzle of this Musgrave Ritual, and it turns out to be a guide to the recovery of a lost family treasure—none other than the crown of King Charles I. It is one of Holmes's most brilliant deductions.

What, then, do we deduce about Eliot's theft of a clue from a detective story for use in a serious work of art about faith, sacrifice, and betrayal? It seems to me that Eliot is offering a hidden tribute and an acknowledgment both to Doyle's genius and to the essence of religion itself—the hidden divinity greater than any tempter sent by any earthly king. The golden crown recovered by Holmes is a kind of metaphor for the treasure within, the secret that lies at the heart of the spiritual search for God.

Even Holmes, not a religious man, is on the search, because he seeks truth. In the passionate pursuit of justice, he is closing in on the secret that is God. God's silence may be "His who is gone"; but, then, so is God "He who will come."

"Mr. Big," with or without a golden crown, is dead. But a subtle God has plenty of disguises to lure us to the treasure within. God for me is so much greater than even the expression "God," the deepest and largest and most expansive word ever devised to direct our heart's attention to the eternal. But it is still not enough. God comes to us shrouded by mystery, not to defeat or to frustrate, but rather to invite us in, to open and free our imaginations and our vision. God is not a king; rather, God is the creative freshness and reality that is the aliveness of all things. We experience this love, this divine intimacy, as being at last closer to us than our own heartbeat, our own breathing. I cannot name this power, but I have felt it over and over—at the birth of each of my three children, and at the deathbed of my mother. These experiences, each a clue to God's shadow, touch us so deeply that we are momentarily lost and caught up in something beyond our thoughts and logic, something so wonderful that words and concepts fail us utterly.

One spiritual master told his disciples that God is the unknown and the unknowable. Bewildered, they asked, "Then why do you talk about God at all?" He shrugged. "Why does a bird sing?"

How, then, can a disappearing God be revealed? In the next chapter, we shall see Holmes in pursuit of something more than justice—the nature of the world itself. When Holmes approaches nature as a scientist, he also approaches this mystery. Pascal says, "All things cover up the same mystery; all things are the veils that cover God." There are other ways for the missing presence to come, other ways for us to sing. God is a silence that answers.

3 * Sherlock Holmes Reads the Book of Life

THE HOLY PASSION of Holmes's for the truth lies in his quest to understand the texture and processes of this world. He is a scientist before he is anything, and he solves "these small problems" he calls Watson's recorded cases because he is in pursuit of a higher mystery.

During an early case Watson walks in on his friend and asks, "Have you solved it?"

"Yes. It was the bisulphate of baryta."

"No, no, the mystery!" Watson cries.

"Oh, that! I thought of the salt that I have been working on."

The scientist in him satisfied, he will then go down to the level of the "mystery" Watson is anxious about, the doings of flawed men and women in an imperfect world. His reply about the case he is working on is typically languid and a touch arrogant: "There was never any mystery in the matter, though, as I said yesterday, some of the details are of interest."

For Holmes, his scientific interests are employed not in the cause of acting as a detective, but very much the other way around. Science and the pursuit of reality's mysteries come first as his inner passion, and the cases sort themselves out by way of his manner of thinking and seeing and experimenting. Yet this book about the quest beyond simply the unknown cannot (Mr. Holmes would not allow it) ignore the searching of science.

It is quite wrong to see science as the slayer of mystery, to assume that as we expose the raw machinery of the cosmos we drain away the sacred qualities of this world in which we find ourselves. Not so. No wonder Holmes has a vision of the unknown which is far greater than the individual cases of justice he can "solve."

But as we shall see, those who wish to read the book of nature as a means of revealing truth will discover that mystery is found not in the things left to be known, but in the range and vastness of all that we do know and all that we can experience. The more we learn, the greater the sense of awe and gratitude. J. Robert Oppenheimer might well have been thinking of the unique figure of the detective, the romancer of reason, when he concluded, "Both the man of science and man of action live always at the edge of mystery, surrounded by it." This edge is ever expanding, ever more alluring. The more science reveals, the greater the edge of mystery revealed as well.

A PROPHET LOOKING BACKWARDS

And why, you might well be asking, would a book about spirituality and the mystery of God suddenly veer off into the realm of scientific wonderment? The answer is that Doyle makes this topic absolutely impossible to ignore. In the very first tale, *A Study in Scarlet*, we are introduced to Holmes in a rather shocking way. Watson's friend Stamford mentions this odd potential roommate as being "a little too scientific for my tastes—it approaches to cold-bloodedness." He even fears Holmes might slip a friend a pinch of a poisonous chemical just to judge its effects. His passion, to Stamford, appears to be for "definite and exact knowledge."

The physician Watson replies, "Very right too."

"Yes, but it may be pushed to excess. When it comes to

beating the subjects in the dissecting-rooms with a stick, it is certainly taking a rather bizarre shape."

"Beating the subjects!" objects Watson, horrified.

"Yes, to verify how far bruises may be produced after death."

Imagine taking the risk of presenting a new hero to readers with the horrifying mental picture of an unfeeling and callous figure whipping corpses with a stick! "Cold-bloodedness," indeed! The scientific sensibility has seldom been presented so directly, the sort of relentless and analytical spirit that echoes Descartes's words to the effect that the task of science was to place nature on the rack to learn her secrets.

But before we condemn science for its adherents' seeming excesses, we need to more properly understand the spirit that underlies this fervent pursuit of the truth, this reading of the world. Mere pages after this daunting introduction of Holmes the scientist, we are given another picture, and this time we will learn that there is a mystical, and nearly religious, vision underlying his relentless scientific quest.

Sitting opposite his new apartment mate (about whom he knows very little, including what this Holmes does for a living), and munching on morning toast, Watson idly picks up a magazine and peruses an article that intrigues and yet annoys him. It is titled "The Book of Life," and Watson finds it quite far-fetched. It presented a process of systematic observation whereby someone well trained in it would be able to know another person's deepest thoughts. It would be impossible, said the writer, to effectively lie to such an astute analytic observer. No wonder this "necromancer" would appear to be a magician!

"What ineffable twaddle," Watson cries, throwing down the magazine. "I never read such rubbish in my life."

Holmes eyes him calmly. "It is evidently the theory of some armchair lounger who evolves all these neat little paradoxes in the seclusion of his own study. It is not practical. I should like to see him clapped down in a third-class carriage on the Underground, and asked to give the trades of all his fellow travelers. I would lay a thousand to one against him."

Then, in a moment whose comedy will be repeated many times to come in the canon, Holmes replies, "You would lose your money. As for the article, I wrote it myself." And here at last Holmes reveals to Watson his profession, that of a detective not connected to the police or the government. This exchange is more than simply comic, and a long passage deserves to be reproduced in full, because it reveals so much of Holmes's vision. The paragraph that so exasperated Watson reads thus:

> From a drop of water, a logician could infer the possibility of an Atlantic or a Niagara without having seen or heard of one or the other. So all life is a great chain, the nature of which is known whenever we are shown a single link of it. Like all the arts, the Science of Deduction and Analysis is one which can only be acquired by long and patient study, nor is life long enough to allow any mortal to attain the highest possible perfection in it. Before turning to those moral and mental aspects of the matter which present the greatest difficulties, let the inquirer begin by mastering more elementary problems. Let him, on meeting a fellow-mortal, learn at a glance to distinguish the history of the man, and the trade and profession to which he belongs. Puerile as such an exercise may seem, it sharpens the faculties of observation, and teaches one where to look and what to look for. By a man's fingernails, by his coat sleeve, by his boots, by his

trouser-knees, by the callosities of his forefinger and thumb, by his expression, by his shirt-cuffs—by each of these things a man's calling is plainly revealed. That all united should fail to enlighten the competent inquirer in any case is almost inconceivable.

Late in his career, Holmes promised to spend his retirement summarizing all his knowledge into a tome to be titled *The Whole Art of Detection.* We have waited nearly a century to see its publication, and only the most faithful of Sherlockians still expect its coming.

No, I am afraid that this paragraph from Holmes's early effort, "The Book of Life," is all we are ever going to possess of the Master's vision direct from his voice (not counting, of course, the somewhat later efforts Holmes himself narrates in a weak imitation of Watson's writings in *The Blanched Soldier* and *The Lion's Mane,* which are better left in the shade).

We know Holmes loves the small details, but we have not yet spied his larger philosophy until we read that pregnant sentence: "So all life is a great chain, the nature of which is known whenever we are shown a single link of it." All it takes is one drop, and an ocean is revealed.

All through the tales, Holmes reinforces this conviction. All nature is interconnected, and all truth is visible from a single link in the chain. A clue is more than a means to a solution to a puzzle—it is a symbol of a way of pursuing truth, a sign pointing to a vision underlying the scientific process. In "The Five Orange Pips," Holmes even expands this, stating that an ideal reasoner should be able to take "a single fact in all its bearings" and be able not only to trace the chain of events leading to that fact, but "also all the results which would follow from it." Past and future both—quite an achievement!

But it is in reasoning backwards that our attention is drawn. Ellery Queen in the novel *The Chinese Orange Mystery* states it a little more clearly: "The detective is a prophet looking backwards." The detective novel is an oddity, in that it moves forward by exposing and demystifying the past. Meaning moves backwards, and the end of the book is meant to return the reader to the beginning, only now with clarity and revelation. What was missing is now found, what was obscure is now clear, and the unknown criminal is now exposed. The detective's peculiar power is in being able to take small pieces of truth (remember that earlier phrase: "Bits of matter matter") and imbue them with such light and thought, place them in a total picture so comprehensive and expansive "in all their bearings," that the detective can "foretell" the past.

"Most people," says the master, "if you describe a train of events to them, will tell you what the results would be. They can put these events together in their minds, and argue from them that something will come to pass. There are few people, however, who, if you told them a result, would be able to evolve from their own inner consciousness what the steps were that led up to that result. This power is what I mean when I talk of reasoning backward."

Holmes speaks as a scientist at the cusp of the twentieth century, living in a time when the theory of evolution is just settling in and, through its general acceptance, changing every aspect of how people viewed their world. He even tells Watson that his technique resembles that of the biologist Cuvier, who could "correctly describe a whole animal by the contemplation of a single bone." In fact, T. H. Huxley, an

early proponent of evolution, called the new scientific method illustrated by the investigation of evolution into the primordial past as "retrospective prophecy."

Readers of the Holmes stories would likely have been familiar with Huxley's popular lecture "On a Piece of Chalk," which takes a humble bit of crumbled chalk and uses it to uncover a vast and complicated prehistory stretching back millions of years. "A small beginning has led us to a great ending," Huxley said, but he could just as well have said that a small ending has led us to a staggering and immense beginning.

Life's great chain is a vast set of interconnected events, and this new vision is not quite the same as the old strict determinism, the view that all events are precisely preordained and ordered—like the bouncing and rebounding of billiard balls on time's table. It is in seeing all things as connected in a stunning chain of events that are complex and interwoven, and thus have to be envisioned as really one event, that we come to understand Holmes's apt phrase, "That all united should fail to enlighten the competent inquirer . . . is almost inconceivable." Truth is not reduced to one simple clue, but a fact found and interpreted "in all its bearings." Reality is "all united."

You and I might or might not spot the clues at a crime scene, but that is only the beginning of the process. We would have to share in a conviction that one piece of evidence is part of an organic whole. The brilliance of detective figures, from Holmes to today's sleuths, is that they do not just see evidence as strictly a product of cause and effect, because this too-linear thinking leads to logical dead ends, mistakes, and fiendishly clever red herrings. Often, the criminal *wants* us to think in this straightforward fashion. In a total system, all bits of matter form a complex picture wherein each clue to the mystery has total relevance to the whole. Says one critic, "For Inspector Lestrade, and for Watson as well, clues can have only one meaning and so either point to an incorrect solution or no solution at all. Holmes, in contrast, operates like a semiotician: he 'reads' crimes like literary texts as if they were systems of signs. The true significance of each sign is determined by its relations to others in a particular network of meaning."

This may sound a little highfalutin, but the bottom line we can all understand: all forms of knowledge must come into play in our search for truth, and this is a search that is not cold-blooded at all, but includes even the mystical. This is a science that, in Holmes's apt word, "enlightens" those who are reading the Book of Life.

To further illustrate the concept of reasoning backwards, several mystery critics have previously focused their attention on Queen's *Chinese Orange* tale. At the core of this mystery novel, a murdered body is found in a room in which everything has been turned upside down or backwards, for example, the victim's clothes. At the crime scene, everything has been inverted or turned around or upside-down, for example, the pictures have been reversed to face the wall. Even a set of Hebrew books has been stolen from the house—books written in Hebrew script, to retain the inverted theme, reading from left to right. The solution to this admittedly absurd mystery lies in the fact that the murderer felt all the clothes of the victim needed to be reversed in order to conceal that he was a priest. Thus the reversed clerical collar could be "hidden" in the wholesale turning about. (Remember when you read a mystery as ornate and convoluted as this that you are really reading a parable closer to a fairy tale than to a modern novel. Remember, as well, Holmes's injunction to never confuse the bizarre with the ultimately mysterious.)

"The whole elaborate if impromptu plan is the handiwork of an artistic murderer, who evidently preferred to turn everything upside down rather than simply reverse the giveaway collar. This is a murderer who has taken pains to make a point about detective logic's backward motion," says David Lehman in *A Perfect Murder*, perhaps the best book ever written about the detective story.

Over and over again, Watson records Holmes's references to this great chain that stretches to the past and beyond, as in *The Valley of Fear*, where Holmes says of Moriarty, "I can see only two things for certain at present—a great brain in London, and a dead man in Sussex. It's the chain between that we are going to trace." It does not matter what the mystery story is, or even the identity of the detective hero or heroine we are following; we are always trying to follow that chain, using the method of reasoning backward.

I have read literally hundreds of mystery novels in the last two years while working on this book, and I discovered one of the most moving illustrations of this principle in the English novelist Peter Ackroyd's *Hawksmoor,* a strange and affecting detective novel that Arthur Conan Doyle would hardly have recognized as such. It is set in present-day London, a very different city from that of Holmes, and as the book opens we find a police detective talking with his assistant about the difficulties they face in solving three murders, or even in determining if they are related. All they know is that two boys and a tramp have been found strangled near one another, and the killings seem to be associated with prominent London churches. They talk of the need to find the story behind the murders, but they don't know where to begin their search.

Says Hawksmoor, the detective, "Yes, the beginning is the tricky part. But perhaps there is no beginning, perhaps we can't look that far back. I never know where anything comes from, Walter."

"Comes from, sir?"

"Where you come from, where I come from, where all this comes from." He stops, embarrassed, "coming to the limits of his understanding." As they prepare to do their duties, the small tasks that can lead to breaking a case open, Hawksmoor sees his profession "as that of rubbing away the grease and detritus which obscured the real picture of the world, in the way that a blackened church must be cleaned before the true texture of its stone can be seen."

Then he realizes that their job is to wait. In reply to his

assistant, Hawksmoor returns to his earlier hope of finding the story behind the murders. "Think of it like a story: even if the beginning has not been understood, we have to go on reading it. Just to see what happens next."

This passion to comprehend the beginning of things is more than a pursuit of logic or reason. It is a profoundly religious impulse, perhaps the most primal and powerful religious instinct there is. Here we find ourselves, in the middle of our lives, hoping to catch on as the story unfolds around us. Perhaps one of the reasons we love the figure of the detective is that she or he can catch, if only for an instant, and if only in a small way, a glimpse of what it must be like to be God and know how everything started, why everything transpired as it did.

Solving a mystery is a way of peering back to the Garden of Eden, or at least to the place where Cain stood, a club in his hand, waiting for the voice of God.

AS BROAD AS NATURE

Soon upon their meeting, when their friendship was just beginning, Watson and Holmes are discussing the power of music, and surprisingly, the authority quoted is Charles Darwin. "He claims that the power of producing and appreciating it existed among the human race long before the power of speech was arrived at," says Holmes. "Perhaps that is why we are so subtly influenced by it. There are vague memories in our soul of those misty centuries when the world was in its childhood."

"That's rather a broad idea," Watson replies.

"One's ideas must be as broad as Nature if they are to interpret Nature."

A scientist takes the details of reality very seriously, and must also possess a vision that will hold that same reality together. As a prophet looking backwards, Holmes dares to look to the origin of things, to where mysteries are born, a single fact with all its bearings, past and future fused, one. All mystery stories are ultimately about reading "the Book of Life." Says the hero of Voltaire's novel *Zadig*, "No one is happier than a philosopher who reads in this great book that God has placed before our eyes." When Holmes is truly in his element, in the middle of an investigation, his attention to "this great book," through its minute details of grass, dirt, and dust, is a kind of meditative trance of complete absorption, like a child in early play. This is happiness of a kind many scientists would readily identify. They know well the truth of Albert Einstein's words, that "the most beautiful thing we can experience is the mysterious. It is the source of all true art and science."

They also identify with the writer of Deuteronomy 30:11–12, where God speaks these encouraging words: "Surely, this instruction . . . is not too baffling for you, nor is it beyond reach. It is not in the heavens, that you should say, 'Who among us can go up to the heavens and get it for us and impart it to us, that we may observe it?' " The mystery of God is not meant to baffle or defeat us; it is not "beyond reach." But on the other hand, this mystery is not something that we dispel or subdue—the mysterious is the very essence of what we reveal as we experience more and more of reality.

It is in this sense that science and religion are complimentary, not antagonistic. We have forgotten that the word *laboratory* in Latin meant a place to work and play. There has always been a religious undergirding to the scientific enterprise, signified by the words chiseled into the gateway of the Cavendish Laboratory in Cambridge, England: "The works of the Lord are great: sought out of all those that have pleasure within."

Science tries to decode the message in the stars, and in our DNA, and in the whorls of a child's fingerprint, and in the rainbow sheen of the most common oil slick, and all the other details of existence. The passion that fuels this search is itself a clue to the nature of who we are. Both science and religion have their own paths to truth, and the means they use to read the Book of Life are different—but the reality that both science and religion point to are one.

How, then, did this conflict of faith and science evolve? Theology, which was once called "the queen of the sciences," has always been a jealous mistress of her approach to truth. Yet from the Enlightenment on, truth has seemingly deserted her and gone to the new suitor, science. Where once science was seen as one great path among many for the pursuit of the truth of God and the scripture of nature, now truth began to be circumscribed to that which could be measured, categorized, labeled, numbered. One by one, on every great dispute concerning the heavens, the age of the earth, the evolution of life (we were once only a little lower than the angels)—wherever religion foolishly tried to fight on the turf of emerging scientific knowledge—theology lost, and lost badly. Thus emerged a sense of the superiority of the scientific viewpoint.

Holmes is clearly a man of this science on the make. He stands firmly in this growing materialistic view—triumphantly so. He dispels mysteries because that appears to be the very essence of scientific enterprise. In fact, some observers of the detective story say that a critical mass of scientifically literate readers had to develop before the genre could become truly popular. The way that Holmes defined reading the Book of Life had to be well on its way to mastery over the old theological vision. While it is true that deductive reasoning has been discovered even in the Bible, as we have seen in the stories of Daniel in the Apocrypha, and in Voltaire's *Zadig*, and in Edgar Allan Poe's groundbreaking 1840 Dupin stories, it is only with Holmes that "reasoning backwards" became a literary sensation, a powerful imaginative tool of creativity and entertainment.

When T. H. Huxley defined the theory of evolution as being "the greatest detective story ever," one suspects Holmes and his physician friend Watson might well have smiled in approval. And the "solution" to this story was going to be, from their sense of having reached the summit of scientific understanding, a triumph for this worldview of materialism and determinism.

But a funny thing happened on the way to the twenty-first century. We now live in a time when mystery has reasserted itself at the very heart of science. Scientists since the quantum revolutions of the 1920s have had to deal with what a church mystic long ago called "The Great Cloud of Unknowing"—a pretty good definition of what is now called the New Physics. Even the comprehensibility of the cosmos is in question, where the realm of Heisenberg's uncertainty principle make modern science more resemble the topsy-turvy paradoxical world of Alice in Wonderland than a tidy Sherlock Holmes story.

When Holmes, in "The Copper Beeches," cries out, "Data! Data! Data! I can't make bricks without clay!" he is surely thinking of Exodus 5:7: "Ye shall no more give the people straw to make brick." Now we have what is termed "quantum ignorance," which means the answers we seek are beyond answering, unanswerable in human terms and thinking. There is now a definable limit to how much data we can collect in reading the Book of Life, even for Mr. Sherlock Holmes. "The Great Cloud of Unknowing" is built right into the subatomic world as an intrinsic principle.

All this would seem to be an affront to reason, except for the fact that reason, good scientific method, got us there. J.B.S. Haldane, one of the great scientists of the century, summed up the new quest for reality with the shocking assessment, "Now my suspicion is that the universe is not only queerer than we suppose, but queerer than we *can* suppose."

Yet as a man of science, Holmes would not be completely at sea amid these changes. After all, he is the one who understood so well that when you have eliminated the impossible, whatever remains, no matter how improbable, must be the truth. Devotion to truth can take you into strange and wondrous territory. Thus our vision is expanded, as broad as nature, as vast as the unimaginable.

FURTHER REVELATIONS

Think again of Watson's criticism of the provocative article written by the young Sherlock Holmes—that "The Book of Life" was a "somewhat ambitious title." Ambitious, indeed! Some critics of the canon have regarded it as being more *blasphemous* than anything else. Readers of the time would have been, I suspect, a little faster to pick up the biblical allusion in this grand title, for the Book of Life appears at the very end of the New Testament, in the book of Revelation.

Probably there has never been a book written as far from

the cool rational sensibility of Sherlock Holmes as the fanatically imagined and vivid dreamwork of Saint John of Patmos's Revelation. You could spend an entire life studying it and hardly get beneath its surreal surface.

At first, I too thought Holmes was simply being audacious in his clear allusion to Revelation, that here in that "ambitious" title was yet another opportunity for the young scientist to show exactly how radical and bohemian he could be. He was willing to have his methods, it seemed, judged alongside that of divine revelation, confident that this method would prove itself superior to such superstitious imagery.

But now I wonder.

Hear the words themselves from Revelation (20:12–15): "And I saw the dead, great and small, standing before the throne, and books were opened. Also another book was opened, which was The Book of Life. And the dead were judged by what was written in the books, by what they had done. And the sea gave up the dead in it, Death and Hades gave up the dead in them, and all were judged by what they had done. Then Death and Hades were thrown in the lake of fire. This is the second death, the lake of fire; and if any one's name was not found written in the Book of Life, he was thrown into the lake of fire."

Think again what Holmes (or any detective) is engaged in. Sometimes, because we tend to read mysteries for entertainment, for mental relaxation, we get a little desensitized to their basic reality: they are about judgment, and the brutal truths of death and mortality. A bloody body in the library is more than an occasion to begin a ritual dance of detection—it is also a *dead* body, and the pursuit of truth is an attempt to bring some resolution and retribution to this violent act that has rent the social fabric and exposed our world as little better and no more advanced than Cain and Abel's.

A person has been slaughtered. It is not only the murderer who will be judged by the quest of the detective, but also the deceased. Secrets will out, and masks be ripped away. Sometimes the dead will be found to be more morally corrupt than the killer.

All "were judged . . . by what they had done." The detective, the prophet looking backwards, forces all of us to look into the Book of Life. Sherlock Holmes is at last more than a dispassionate scientist, an experimenter with blood under his gaze. A man who looks into the lake of fire must be a person of vision, able to see "all united," as Holmes says—back even to the place of origin, where the message and the meaning of this world were one. To see the world with unflinching eyes, to see it truly and with the fortitude to steer toward the truth, no matter how twisted and dismaying it proves, is never easy. No wonder, then, that Holmes sometimes seeks relief from the pain and sordid reality of his investigations in the serene relief of pure scientific research. In "The Final Problem," he tells Watson, "Of late I have been tempted to look into the problems furnished by nature rather than those more superficial ones for which our artificial state of society is responsible." It will be more than a decade before Holmes achieves this goal, to retire to his Sussex farmhouse, there to enjoy his "philosophical" endeavors. And in the meantime, this man of science would be faced with challenges of the highest order, not only to his skill as a detective, but to his identity as a rational man.

4 * No Ghosts Need Apply

HOLMES IS A MAN OF FAITH, all right—faith that there is always a natural, not a supernatural, explanation.

Near the end of his career he is sent a letter with the intriguing reference: "Re: Vampires." Thus is he drawn into a sordid and sad tale of secrets and hidden jealousies in a Sussex family in which it appears that a young baby has been the victim of a mother cursed with vampirism. But Watson has set the tale up for us in such a way that we are wary of any such conclusion. Before setting out for the countryside to begin the investigation of "The Sussex Vampire," Holmes pulls down one of the heavy volumes of clippings he maintains, and under *V* he reads of vampires in Hungary and Transylvania. At last, he throws down the collection "with a snarl of disappointment."

"Rubbish, Watson, rubbish! What have we to do with walking corpses who can only be held in their grave by stakes driven through their hearts? It's pure lunacy."

Watson replies that vampires need not be the dead, but the living. "I have read, for example, of the old sucking the blood of the young in order to retain their youth."

"You are right, Watson. It mentions the legend in one of these references. But are we to give serious attention to such things? This agency stands flat-footed upon the ground, and there it must remain." Then he says words that are emblematic of his essential life philosophy: "The world is big enough for us. No ghosts need apply."

There is a strong instinct that he appears to be indifferent to, and at times nearly contemptuous of, and that is the allure of the supernatural, the miraculous, and the occult. Holmes's distrust (nearly distaste) of the supernatural could well be illustrated by a story told of Thoreau on his deathbed. A minister friend, speaking to him about his coming death, asked, "You seem so near the brink of the dark river that I wonder how the opposite shore may appear to you."

The naturalist whispered back, "One world at a time."

It seems detectives too can only deal with one world at a time, and what is hidden from them comes not from the agency of angels, goblins, devils, or any other supernatural explanation. When something appears to be from beyond this world, Holmes is sure that a more cunning intelligence is at work *in this world.* If there exists an opportunity to hear the harmony of "the higher heavenly world," then Holmes is steadfastly deaf to it. And when evil rears its grinning and horrid face, Holmes always spies a human visage behind the mask.

Yet one of the most intriguing mysteries to be found in this book is this: that at the very same time Arthur Conan Doyle was publishing this story (in 1924), he was becoming known all around the world for his advocacy of Spiritualism! Doyle, having traveled by then more than fifty thousand miles and spoken to more than a quarter of a million people about the proof of life after death and life beyond our senses, was perhaps the last man to be represented by a fictional character who believed that this world is large enough for us without life after death and all the ineffable powers that impinge on our lives. For the realm of spirit-rappings, seances, the photographing of fairies, and the voices of the dead speaking from the beyond there was no more articulate and courageous spokesman than Doyle.

What a strange irony that Doyle's long and deeply controversial campaign (which could have been summed up as "ghosts may indeed apply") was principally financed by the sales of none other than that utterly rational and thoroughly skeptical Sherlock Holmes.

Doyle used his fame as the creator of Holmes and the master of the detective story to entice reporters to publicize the cause of Spiritualism, and audiences would crowd lecture halls to hear him simply because they loved the great detective. Biographers have struggled for decades to understand and somehow resolve this strange paradox, but they have ended up largely throwing up their hands in befuddlement. How could this decent, charming, but clearly addled and overly credulous true believer possibly have invented and given such vivid life to a character like Holmes? We shall see that there may be, in fact, a resolution to this admittedly odd situation.

Maybe his biographers, drawn to him because of their love of Sherlock Holmes, have never properly understood Doyle's own complex and fascinating personal spiritual quest. Perhaps part of this mystery's solution lies in the fact that the religious parables contained within the Holmes stories have been so cunningly masked.

A CASE FOR A POLICEMAN OR A CLERGYMAN?

Ask the most devoted fans of Holmes what is their favorite story, and there is no question which they would select.

Ask a reader indifferent to mystery novels as to which Sherlock Holmes story he would be most likely to read, and the answer would be the same.

Ask a movie producer which Holmes story is the most dramatic and thrilling to film, and film again.

Ask a mystery writer which story she wishes she had written, and the answer once again, and always, will be *The Hound of the Baskervilles*. This is the place where for Doyle everything fell into place—a rich and complex plot, plenty of cunning twists and surprises, a splendidly realized locale in the dreary moors of Dartmoor, and a tale in which the great Sherlock Holmes fits in without utterly dominating the story. Yet the reason I think we revere *The Hound* as not simply the best Holmes tale but perhaps the greatest detective novel ever written is something simpler.

It is the haunting, gothic feeling of dread that pervades the whole story that draws us in. There is in the writing a sure and confident handling of the hovering suspense of the supernatural. This is really Holmes at his finest, fighting not against any mere criminal but against the specter of evil itself. It is all we can do to resist succumbing to the reality of a supernatural curse in the horrific guise of a bounding spectral hound springing at our very own throats. This is a test not merely of Holmes's intellect but of his inner dedication to the intelligence of this world, nothing less than his own ordering of what is at last true.

As Sir Henry Baskerville says bravely when the dangers of his reclaiming his legacy of Baskerville Hall are presented to him, "You don't seem quite to have made up your mind whether it's a case for a policeman or a clergyman." The sense that this curse is absolutely real is what makes the novel such a perfect illustration of the particular ethos of the detective novel—that the world can make sense only by reference to the realities of *this* world. The brilliance of *The Hound of the Baskervilles* is in its keenly balanced contest between the supernatural view of the world and the scientific, materialist view.

The facts of the case are presented to us by way of a long prologue, in which Holmes torments Watson, as usual, for his inability to correctly draw deductions from the physical appearance of an object, in this case Dr. John Mortimer's walking stick. When Mortimer finally arrives, he is presented as a person "of precise mind." Mortimer adds, describing himself, that he is "A dabbler in science, Mr. Holmes, a picker up of shells on the shores of the great unknown ocean." (This is an allusion to the famous quote of Isaac Newton, made when he was an old man looking back at his lifetime of achievement in assessing the physical nature of reality.) The story Mortimer brings to 221-B Baker Street is the more shocking coming from this figure who would appear to Holmes and Watson a thoroughly credible and scientifically minded source.

It seems that Sir Charles Baskerville has been found brutally murdered in strange circumstances. The novel's second chapter, in which the particulars of his death are described, ends with words that have justly been called the best cliffhanger sentences in literature. Near the body there were found an odd set of footprints. Holmes asks if they were a man's or a woman's. Then comes the kicker: "Mr. Holmes, they were the footprints of a gigantic hound!"

As the details of this horrible death are revealed, this inner contest between rationality and the supernatural begins to build. Mortimer reluctantly hesitates, and then ventures, "There is a realm in which the most acute and experienced of detectives is helpless."

"You mean that the thing is supernatural?"

"I did not positively say so."

"No, but you evidently think it."

Mortimer admits that his perspective has been shaken by several reports of things beyond "the settled order of Nature." He goes on: "I find that before the terrible event occurred several people had seen a creature upon the moor which corresponds with this Baskerville demon, and which could not possibly be any animal known to science. They all agreed that it was a huge creature, luminous, ghastly, and spectral." Holmes asks him directly, as a man of science, if he believes it to be of this earth. Dr. Mortimer confesses he is not sure.

To this, Holmes shrugs, then adds, "I have hitherto confined my investigations to this world. In a modest way I have combated evil, but to take on the Father of Evil himself, would, perhaps, be too ambitious a task." Why this is too "ambitious" is stated by Holmes pretty clearly when he concludes that young Henry Baskerville, Sir Charles's nephew and heir, would be just as safe in Dartmoor as in London, since the agency of such an evil could not be localized, and that if it is not material in nature (though Holmes takes pains to establish that the hound's footprints were material, as were the wounds effected by the "spectral beast"), then no detecting would be possible.

Holmes reinforces this perspective when he speaks with Watson hours later, after he has had a good pipe and pondered this peculiar case. He says to Watson, "If the devil did desire to have a hand in the affairs of men—" but he is interrupted by his friend.

"Then you are yourself inclining to the supernaturalist explanation."

Holmes retorts, "The devil's agents may be of flesh and blood, may they not?" Then he sums up what they are fac-

ing if they proceed to investigate the supposed curse on the Baskerville family: "Of course, if Dr. Mortimer's surmise should be correct, and we are dealing with forces outside the ordinary laws of Nature, there is an end of our investigations. But we are bound to exhaust all other hypotheses before falling back on that one."

This is but a variation on Holmes's famous dictum from *The Sign of Four*, spoken after Holmes and Watson discover the murdered body of Thaddeus Sholto in a room that has been locked and is accessible only by a small hole in the roof. When the mystery seems the darkest and most perplexing to Watson, Holmes takes the only route out. "How often have I said to you that when you have eliminated the impossible, whatever remains, *however improbable*, must be the truth?"

The key here, and why detective fiction cannot operate in a world where the supernatural is admitted, is Holmes's strict elimination of "the impossible." There have been a few efforts to include the supernatural in detective fiction, notably Randall Garrett's "Lord Darcy" stories and more recently, the Sir Adam Sinclair "Adept" series by Katherine Kurtz and Deborah Turner Harris, but even here, the powers of magic and the miraculous are sharply circumscribed and turned into yet one more means of finding order in our material world. Here the supernatural powers employed by detective and villain alike are really powers of the mind that science has not yet learned to measure or control, but are really just an extension of our normal mental processes. In these "supernatural" detective novels, the world of magic is revealed—as it originally was in the time of the early alchemists, and all the way up to the time of Newton (who himself did secret work in the occult)—as being a kind of technology of largely untapped mental powers.

The world of the truly miraculous would render void any effort on the part of the sleuth to rationally reach back to the origins of truth for one simple reason: if this realm of reality were admitted into our thinking, we would also be forced to see it as arbitrary, capricious, and, to our thinking minds at least, incomprehensible. This would be a realm of mystery that the mystery novel could never enter.

For Holmes, where the "however improbable" takes us is not into the world of the impossible (the supernatural), but into the shrouded and twisted mind of the criminal who has forced us to confront, quite literally, "the devil's agents of flesh and blood." Evil is not magical; it is all too human, no matter how ingenious or glittering in its reasoning and cunning. In the contest of good and evil, the rational must and will forever reign supreme. One writer on Doyle, Martin Ebon, notes that Holmes "looks, in retrospect, like an antidote to the occult, an oasis of reliable, materialistic order. There are no spirit rappings on the walls of his house in Baker Street."

In tales such as "The Sussex Vampire," "The Devil's Foot," and *The Hound of the Baskervilles,* Doyle maintains a tension between our wanting to believe in the reality of the supernatural and our belief in the supremacy of reason over superstition. Then, at the last possible moment, this finely drawn tension is resolutely shattered by the stunning revelations of Holmes. Hundreds of detective stories have henceforth followed this model, especially in classic "locked-room" murder stories where there seems to be no logical explanation for the horrific results other than the powers of the demonic. Yet over and over, these detectives whom Holmes has inspired manage to find the fatal flaw in the all-too-human plans of these criminals who only *pose* as other-worldly.

The well-made detective story can be seen not as a realistic novel but more as a catalogue of magic tricks wherein we willingly suspend belief in the normal laws of physics—except that, in the code of the genre, the magician (the writer) must step forward at the conclusion to shatter the illusion and explain how it was all done. Unlike the case of a magic show, where the illusion remains unbroken as we file out of the theater, we cannot close the book and have this suspension of belief in the impossible maintained. We must be returned to the world of cause and effect, of reason and resolution. If your detective solves the case by employing spectacular powers of ESP, or by looking into a crystal ball, or by attending a seance in which the victim reveals the murderer through a medium, then you have not read a detective novel. You may have mystery, but not one solved by the process of deduction.

Our pleasure in reading Sherlock Holmes comes from living in this precise and circumscribed world of reason, but *all the time* being tempted and titillated by the impossible, the miraculous, the enigmatic. It must be a close-run thing, and Doyle, so attuned to Spiritualism, knew exactly how to spin this web of intrigue and mounting tension. The solution must be simple, surprising, and utterly plausible. "Why didn't I guess that?" we should be compelled to think, and if the author is being fair (and Doyle sometimes was not, making Holmes privy to some piece of the puzzle he did not share with Watson, nor thus with us), we could have. We do not have to possess sensitive spiritual gifts, only a functioning brain.

The pleasure of the mystery story is in this cracking open of mystery, the collapse of this willing investment in the dreamlike hope that maybe, just once, *the solution really will be revealed as miraculous.* But no, that is only a teasing and momentary longing. By the last page, we want our world returned to order and regularity. The detective is like the mystic who, as detective writer G. K. Chesterton once paradoxically maintained, is no mere dreamer but precisely the one who reveals truth, not conceals it. The mystic, he said, "does not bring doubts and riddles: the doubts and riddles exist already. . . . The mystic is not the man who makes mysteries, but the one who destroys them." Chesterton concluded, then, that the successful detective writer is not the one who baffles the reader but who uses the slow and imaginative revelation of the tale "to enlighten the reader."

THE EXACT SCIENCE OF RELIGION

We met with an interesting paradox in the previous chapter, where scientific method was revealed as the path to quantum mystery. Well, like unto it, here is another winsome paradox: sometimes spirituality is precisely the path to the highest form of reason and rationality. Let's recall those words of Holmes's from the beginning of this book, when he says in "The Naval Treaty": "There is nothing in which deduction is so necessary as in religion. It can be built up as an exact science by the reasoner."

This seems so paradoxical, but although religion at its highest, most universal, and most compassionate may transcend reason, may rise above and beyond human terms and definitions, *it does not contradict or nullify reason.*

Here is why Holmes is wise to call religion "an exact science." Reason and order, after all, must lie at the heart of the religious quest for final and primal truth. God is a truth we may never comprehend, but the heart of reality cannot be arbitrary or mere chaos. To be religious is to have faith in the intelligence of this reality, and to trust that this intelligibility is at last to be known in the experience of love, of mercy, of a cosmic compassion. Father Brown, the priest in the detective tale *The Head of Caesar,* says it well: "What we all dread most is a maze with no center. That is why atheism is only a nightmare." (The detective Lew Archer in *The Instant Enemy* is left looking at a painting by Klee, and as he stares at the modern canvas, he reflects, "The man was in the maze, the maze was in the man.") God may be apprehended in the twining labyrinth of mystery, but true labyrinths lead somewhere; they take us on a journey. Indeed, the use of the ancient labyrinth is enjoying a resurgence today as a spiritual tool of discovery.

In the very first Father Brown story, *The Blue Cross,* a false priest (really a master criminal intent upon stealing a sapphire cross) is unexpectedly foiled. When he demands to know how Father Brown knew he was not what he seemed, the bland little priest replies, "Another part of my trade, too, made me sure you weren't a priest."

"What?" asks the astonished thief.

"You attacked reason. It's bad theology."

In an earlier conversation with the priest on Hampstead Heath, the criminal had wondered if there might not be other universes where our reason would appear unreasonable. Brown had stoutly replied that reason is the same anywhere, even "in the last limbo, in the lost borderland of things." He goes on to add words that should shock only those who accept religion in its most basic form: "I know that people charge the Church with lowering reason, but it is just the other way. Alone on earth, the Church makes reason really supreme. Alone on earth, the Church affirms that God Himself is bound by reason."

Mystery in the religious sense is not a puzzle to be solved, but an aspect of reality to be fully experienced and realized. This does not mean turning off our minds! Indeed, to confront the mysteries of life does not mean to throw up our hands and say, "Some things are just unknowable," or "Some things are beyond our sight." Gordon Kaufman, a professor of mine at the Harvard Divinity School, says very simply that mystery "refers to bafflement of mind more than obscurity of perception."

It does not mean that mystery is not present and right before our eyes, in every aspect of our lives from birth to death, and perhaps beyond. It is just that this reality is intrinsically hard, if not impossible, for our limited brains to wrap around. Luckily, there is dimension of truth that cannot be measured or defined, and we touch it in dance, in ritual, in music, in poetry, in art, and, when all these things are combined, in religion.

Religion is, in this limited sense, the science of mystery. She is still the queen of the sciences. Science as currently and historically understood can only take reason so far.

Religious language contains its own sense of reason, because we at last face the very limits of our ability to reason. Here at the edge of reason, it is only reasonable to begin to employ the language of mystery and faith. This is not a hidden appeal to unreason in religious faith, nor an attempt to justify crazy emotions in the name of faith, but something a bit more subtle. Stay with me just a little further. Listen to Gordon Kaufman again, when he says mystery "calls attention to something about ourselves: that we seem to have reached a limit to our powers at this point, and may, if we are not careful, easily become confused or misled." Thus, when we call something "mysterious" it is a very important signal that "special rules" in our use of language should now be followed: take unusual care, beware of what is being said (or not said).

Then he concludes with words that shook me when I first confronted them: "When we introduce the concept of mystery into our theological work, this does not mean that we may now cease employing our faculties in a thoroughly critical way. On the contrary, it alerts us to the necessity at this point to employ our critical capacities to their utmost."

In the Upanishads, it is written: "He truly knows Brahaman who knows him as beyond knowledge; he who knows things that he knows, knows not. The ignorant think that Brahaman is known, but the wise know him to be beyond knowledge."

The Jews refused to even allow the name of God to be spoken or written, such was their caution with God's majestic mystery.

In the Tao Te Ching it is written: "Those who know do not speak, and those who speak do not know" (terrifying words for a preacher to quote).

And Jesus warned his followers about being manipulated after his death (Luke 21:8–9): "Take heed that you are not led astray; for many will come in my name, saying 'I am he!' and 'The time is at hand!' Do not go after them."

Discernment is being asked of us. Thus great religious leaders have offered caution as well as vision. I well remember going to a conference on spiritual autobiography led by the writer Sam Keen. I was amused (and some were shocked) when Keen said, "The one thing you need to pack in your bag for the spiritual journey is a good Bull Shit detector." Yes, it certainly helps, and here we find another way of saying, "Watch out—mystery is around the bend. Pay attention and be especially careful now."

Doyle, who ended up a Spiritualist, is a pretty good guide to the caution signs along the way, and I believe the "supernatural" tales of Holmes were meant to help us, besides showing us a rattling good time, to be utterly cautious and clear when facing the ineffable—as each of us surely will in our lives. "But the Almighty law," said Doyle, "is that we must use our own brains, and find our own salvation; and it is not made too easy for us."

NOT NECESSARILY THE NEW AGE

One of the later stories in the canon is the underrated and seldom reviewed tale of terror called "The Adventure of the Devil's Foot." Exhausted from overwork and unspecified "occasional indiscretions," Holmes has gone to the Cornish peninsula to vacation with his friend. But there is no rest for the detective, for one of the conventions of the detective genre is that murder always seems to follow the detective, not vice versa. Sure enough, they are quickly presented with the shocking scene of a dead woman, two of her brothers seated next to her, both of whom have been driven mad—all apparently the victims of something so horrible and shocking that the vicar, Mr. Roundhay, and his tenant, Mr. Mortimer Tregennis, when describing the circumstances, have no recourse but to ascribe the cause to something demonic.

"It is devilish, Mr. Holmes, devilish!" cries Tregennis, brother to the three afflicted. "It is not of this world. Something has come into that room which has dashed the light of reason from their minds. What human contrivance could do that!"

Holmes replies, "I fear that if the matter is beyond humanity it is certainly beyond me. Yet we must exhaust all natural explanations before we fall back upon such a theory as this." He later remarks to Watson during a private walk, "I take it, in the first place, that neither of us is prepared to admit diabolical intrusions into the affairs of men. Let us begin by ruling that entirely out of our minds."

As it turns out, Holmes's suppositions are well taken; for the devil at the heart of the solution of this ghastly mystery is the one mentioned in the title, "the devil's foot," a rare and dangerous powder ground from a root that "is shaped like a foot, half-human, half goatlike. . . ." This drug is used as an ordeal poison by medicine men and induces madness or death. Diabolical it is, but not demonic.

I sometimes think of Holmes's skepticism and his admonition to "exhaust all natural explanations" when I am exposed to the effusions and exuberant enthusiasms of what is loosely called the New Age movement. Without clergy, churches, denominational bureaucrats, or hierarchical structures, this spiritual tidal wave is reshaping the religious landscape. Like a brightly colored carnival, it has rolled into town with its gaudy sideshows of channeling, crystals, astrology, astral-traveling, reincarnation, holistic healing, alien abductions, healing, ESP, and gurus galore. While I regard this movement as being largely a positive, even hopeful phenomenon, there is little about it that is either new or novel, and there is much about it that calls for a bit of Holmes's caution and rigorous introspection. The appeal of the supernatural, even in this age of the seeming triumph of scientific materialism, seems to be an intrinsic aspect of the human mind, and it need not be attached to organized religion.

But what has any of this to do with Sherlock Holmes or his creator?

In trying to resolve the paradox of a Spiritualist having created, in Holmes, the ultimate symbol of scientific skepticism, I discovered something surprising—that Doyle, this mild-mannered doctor turned popular writer, was really a precursor of the New Age movement, almost its patron saint. The many thousands of people who are today leaving behind their established religions to find a more eclectic and universalized spiritual path are retracing a path that Doyle pioneered a century before. In short, the New Age movement may perhaps be better understood as simply another wave of a perennial religious instinct to try to recapture the personal experience of the spark of divine reality within.

This was the meaning of the Transcendental movement of Thoreau and Emerson and Carlyle, the last of whom Holmes praises and quotes in the stories. When organized religion loses its vitality and deep connection to the personal experience of divinity, when it forgets, denies, or represses this spiritual freshness and creativity, other forces and vibrant energies will arise. This movement is not a rejection of religion, but rather a reform of it, and a part of the continuing revolution in spiritual transformation. But in the midst of all this upheaval, both positive and less positive aspects of faith can intertwine in great confusion (and sometimes with less than sensible results). Spiritual discernment is just as necessary as spiritual enthusiasm, and both should be seen as gifts of God.

Here is Doyle's story:

He was born in Edinburgh, into a strict Roman Catholic family, and educated in Jesuit schools. Yet by the time he entered medical school, he had begun to reject certain aspects of that faith. At the Stonyhurst School in Lancaster, England, he remembered hearing a "great fierce Irish priest" blast to damnation all those who were not Roman Catholic. "I looked upon him with horror; all that was sanest and most generous in my nature rose up against a narrow theology and an uncharitable outlook upon the other great religions of the world."

This feeling, compounded by his exposure to the ideas of Darwin and other radical thinkers, shook his faith. He slowly became an agnostic, though never quite an atheist. The certainties of faith now were replaced by a lifelong quest for something else, something new. He studied other religions and had a broad sympathy for the search for God beyond strict definitions and creeds.

He even published, in 1895, a sort of spiritual autobiography, *The Stark Munro Letters*, a book seldom read today. It is still an amusing and at times poignant novel, and it certainly illuminates Doyle's adventurous attitude toward this spiritual search. Stark Munro, a young doctor (who clearly represents Doyle himself), writes to a friend: "Is religion the only domain of thought which is non-progressive, and to be referred forever to a standard set two thousand years ago? Can they not see as the human brain evolves it must take a wider outlook? A half-formed brain makes a half-formed God. . . ."

This search for faith was not a contradiction of his love of science and reason. He felt they went together, as both were servants of truth. "I do not admit that any faith—but only pure reason—is needed to get the idea of God and also to evolve a sufficient moral law for our needs." His "broad Theism" allowed him to state, twenty years after writing the book, that "I have kept my mind very open and have read much and thought much on the subject. . . ."

So, the picture of Doyle that emerges here is not of a credulous innocent tumbling into Spiritualism but of a man whose spiritual quest was really a form of the scientific method. Above all, he felt, it was necessary to somehow end the savage and intolerant warfare between religions. He had a vision that "the end and aim of spiritual intercourse is . . . to found the grand religion of the future." This quality is what finally made Spiritualism attractive to Doyle, since it rose above and beyond any one faith and yet offered (it seemed to him, at any rate) a sound experiential basis for faith. It took him many years to fully convert to the Spiritualist vision and accept the means of the medium to communicate with the dead, and when he did, he insisted that he did so as a practical, tough-minded searcher for evidence. He would face his critics and state, "When I add that I am a Doctor of medicine, specially trained in observation, and that as a public man of affairs I have never shown myself to be wild and unreasonable, I hope I have persuaded you that my opinion should have some weight as compared with those opponents whose contempt for the subject has been so great that it has prevented them from giving calm consideration to the facts."

He did not have to add that as the father of Sherlock Holmes, he could "out-skepticize" any of his critics, and that is perhaps why, in the end, he retained Holmes. In the battles he was embroiled in near the end of his life, Holmes was the last card he had left to play to convince others of his credibility, and that he knew what was, and what was not, evidence worth considering. He did convert one fictional character, the scientist Professor Challenger (whom you might remember from Doyle's *The Lost World*, from which Michael Crichton lifted the title and plot for his own dinosaur book); but Holmes he kept above the fray, the scientific man extraordinaire. Whether one agrees with Doyle or not concerning the truth of Spiritualism, it does him a grand disservice to see him as a foolish and naïve man. While I do not happen to share his Spiritualist beliefs, I find myself admiring his Universalist hope for religion, and his sense that the faith of the future must, and will, ally itself securely with the gains of science. This optimistic view of the progress of faith he called "the science of religion."

It is easy to make light of his acceptance of fairy photography, or to side with his friend Houdini in the investigation of fraudulent mediums, but to his dying day, Doyle was convinced that a new world religion that was compatible with science and personal experience was possible, and was in fact present in the movement he so loved. He called Spiritualism "the first attempt ever made in modern times to support faith by actual provable fact."

I suspect there are many people today, believers in the supernatural or otherwise, who might well identify with the spiritual journey of Doyle. His life is a microcosm of the New Age movement today, in both its positive and negative aspects. In the end, Holmes is Doyle's alter ego (and perhaps also his altar ego), addressing the too-easy thrill of the supernatural along with the necessity to ground one's faith in a firm reality that we should expect—and wish—to be tested. To apply reason and caution in the realm of mystery may be the most useful religious writing Doyle ever did.

Most modern spiritual pilgrims, and I count myself among them, possess both a deep hunger for a fresh and creative faith and an equally strong need not to be fooled or manipulated. We want a faith that is not being propped up with rickety tales of miracles and tinseled visions. We want a faith a little closer to the ground, something that seems threaded into the realm of the everyday and the ordinary, not the grand and the glittering.

Saint Paul was trying to convey something of this when he wrote to the new church in Corinth, whose members were all excited about who had the greatest and most spectacular of spiritual gifts and miraculous powers. He said these gifts were ultimately not very important in God's eyes; that compassion and love and mercy would be the hallmarks of a true faith, what he called "the higher gifts," not these supernatural effusions. After his great hymn to love, Paul adds (1 Cor. 14:14–15): "For if I pray in a tongue, my spirit prays but my mind is unproductive. What can I do? I will pray with the spirit and I will pray with the mind also. . . ."

As the years have passed in my own ministry, I grow more open to the miraculous, more attuned to the odd and strange things that happen to all of us (even the eternally skeptical Unitarian-Universalists I serve), the experiences

that can shake up a narrowly scientific world view. But I also grow equally convinced that, in this time of the supposed New Age, God's mystery is revealed much more powerfully in the humble and subtle observations of daily life than in all the wonders and great claims of power from the beyond. The here and now is already wonder-filled beyond our reckoning, and if it is the eternally skeptical Mr. Sherlock Holmes who can teach me that, then I will take my parables wherever I can find them.

There is really no mystery in the creator of Holmes searching for life after death. Let Christopher Morley have the last, and wisest, word: "But there was no stage of the life, from the poor student doing without lunch to buy books, to the famous author enduring painful hostility for his psychic faith, which did not reflect the courage, the chivalry, the sagacity we would have expected from the creator of Holmes. Certainly it was characteristic of that student of mysteries to attack the greatest one we know."

It is also characteristic for the mystery novel to attack the great citadel of death, that vast riddle of our mortality and our fragility, and it is to this ultimate expedition that we now turn.

5 * God's Spies

WE ARE HALFWAY through the case of "The Red-Headed League," and Watson is totally befuddled. A case that has up to now had overtones of comic absurdity has suddenly opened into a baffling criminal conspiracy that it seems only Holmes can envision. After checking out the stores of Saxe Coburg Square and the dirty knees of the assistant of Mr. Jabez Wilson, their slightly foolish red-headed client, Holmes is asked by Watson, "And what did you see?"

"What I expected to see."

"Why did you beat the pavement?"

"My dear doctor, this is a time for observation, not for talk." Then he speaks words that strike to the heart of the mystery tale: "We are spies in an enemy's country."

Through the detective, we can exercise our lust for other's secrets, peering into the guilt of others "in an enemy's country." When preparing for this book, I was obligated to take monthly three-hour bus trips to meetings in Boston, so over a year I used the opportunity to read and reread every page of the Holmesian canon. I well remember reading this passage and pausing to look out to the foggy early-morning landscape as we rolled along the Massachusetts Turnpike. Something stirred in me, a dim memory from a fugitive reading, something from my college years. Then it came—King Lear, now a prisoner and coming to the end of his raging madness, speaks to his daughter Cordelia:

> *So we'll live,*
> *And pray, and sing, and tell old tales, and laugh*

At gilded butterflies, and hear poor rogues
Talk of court news; and we'll talk with them too:
Who loses and who wins, who's in, who's out;
And take upon's the mystery of things,
As if we were God's spies . . .

—act 5, scene 3

I had the sure sense that Doyle was thinking of this passage when he had Holmes tell Watson of their role as spies in their effort to find guilt—"Who loses and who gains, who's in, who's out." Anyone who takes on this harrowing task is entering into a dangerous realm, to take upon themselves "the mystery of things." Being one of God's spies is a precarious and perilous role, poised above either triumph or disaster, not really knowing if one is doing the work of angels or that of demons. It is hard sometimes to know the difference.

In *The Catalogue of Crime*, the word *detection* is defined by Jacques Barzun and Wendell Hertig Taylor with the following entry:

> [Detection] means 'taking the roof off,' i.e., uncovering what is hidden. In the Spanish literary tradition, the Devil occasionally offered one of his favorites the entertainment of looking into all the houses of a town by taking the roofs off. Detectives are consequently sons or disciples of the Devil.

We are so accustomed to thinking of the detective in positive terms, especially when we think of the gentlemanly Sherlock Holmes, that we do not often stop to consider that these stories, fables though they be, expose the darkest and least noble aspect of human behavior. Mystery stories show our nature in its most brutal and elemental form, with all our roofs torn off and the Devil's work exposed.

THE STATE OF EDEN

Probably the greatest essay ever written about detective fiction was by the poet W. H. Auden, whose "The Guilty Vicarage" is a model of graceful (and shrewd) literary insight and theological depth. In it he maintains that the mystery story is a kind of fantasy in which we can feel safely isolated from guilt and the chaos of evil, and this illusion is sustained by the almost supernatural abilities of the detective, who brings an Eden-like order back to society—and to us, the readers. "The job of the detective," notes Auden, "is to restore the state of grace in which the aesthetic and the ethical are one. Since the murderer who caused their disjunction is the aesthetically defiant individual, his opponent, the detective, must be . . . the exceptional individual who is himself in a state of grace."

He goes on to observe that "Holmes is the exceptional individual who is in a state of grace because he is a genius in whom scientific curiosity is raised to the status of a heroic passion." Well and good, and one can certainly plausibly maintain that we love mystery tales because we can tell ourselves that we are safely in the corner of goodness, truth, and right, along with our hero or heroine, and who can argue that Holmes is indeed a genius in a kind of "state of grace"?

The only problem with this quite sensible assertion comes from one suggestive sentence in Auden's essay. "I suspect," adds Auden, one of the great literary figures of our century, "that the typical reader of detective stories is, like myself, a person who suffers from a sense of sin." Exactly. Even though we struggle to entertain this pleasant illusion of "being disassociated from the murderer," it is just that, an illusion, and a not very convincing one at that.

Arguing against this too-simple appeal of "disassociation" are the many suggestions threaded throughout detective stories that to be God's spy is to be bound up and haunted with guilt in the most intimate of ways.

Even the noble Holmes, whether in a state of grace or not, is presented to us as a person perilously close to evil. Watson even thinks to himself as he watches his friend investigate *The Sign of Four*, "So swift, silent, and furtive were his movements, like those of a trained bloodhound picking out a scent, that I could not but think what a terrible criminal he would have made had he turned his energy and sagacity against the law. . . ." In fact, one of the weirdest experiences of close reading of the canon is to be struck by the disturbing similarity in the way Doyle describes both his hero and his most nefarious and brilliant foe, Professor Moriarty.

In "The Final Problem," Watson is finally informed by Holmes of Moriarty's villainy, and how his evil vision lies behind so much heretofore unexplained crime. "He is the Napoleon of crime . . . a genius, a philosopher, an abstract thinker. He has a brain of the first order. He sits motionless, like a spider in the center of its web, but that web has a thousand radiations, and he knows well every quiver of each of them." Yet in a later tale, Watson will note that Holmes "loved to lie in the very centre of five millions of people, with his filaments stretching out and running through them, responsive to every little rumour or suspicion of unsolved crime."

What, then, have we here? Perhaps nothing more than a poetic image Doyle forgot he had already used once before—but somehow I doubt it. Here is a powerful suggestion that there is a bond, a kind of doppelganger twinning of hunted and hunter, between dark and light, between criminal and sleuth. And, as well, an intimation that there is an astonishingly thin line between these opposites, these opponents who are playing, after all, the same game.

Auden maintained that the primary appeal of the mystery story is the fantasy that we can return to the Garden of Eden. To me, the issue is murkier and a little more complex. The detective serves as our agent as we enter the realms of moral confusion or utter depravity, and through this agent we allow ourselves to hold up a mirror to truly see ourselves, if only for a moment, in the safe ordered world of fiction.

What we see there could hardly be called innocence.

THE GUILTY PARTY

There, in the mirror of the parables of detective fiction, we allow ourselves to realize we are capable of such acts, yet also, through the magic of fiction, as beings able to "solve" and redeem the worst within ourselves. If any of this sounds familiar, it is. This is, as I understand it, the very core of healing and spiritual realization as found in many religious traditions. We cannot grow in faith entertaining the fantasy that we are innocent beings, perfect and angelic. No, the path to God is much stonier than this and requires that we see and identify the worst in ourselves, the pain and the wreckage, and deal forthrightly with it. If we do not confront the shadow within ourselves, we find that the light of God recedes from us. This is just the way it is, and mature people face up to it. James Gillis, in *The Church and Modern Thought*, writes: "The deepest and strangest mysteries, the weirdest and most wonderful, the most shocking and most sublime, are those that even after all these aeons lie concealed in the dark and tortuous depths of the mind of man."

Or as the wise detective Brother Cadfael says to a fellow monk, "You'll never get to be a saint if you deny the bit of the devil in you."

A little haunting by guilt is not only good for you, but utterly necessary for us to see ourselves honestly. It is a necessary spiritual tool if we are to see ourselves as bound to others, as beings imperfect and equal to others in their pain and confusion. We all have to become God's spies, not in an enemy's country but in a terrain we are all too familiar with, the landscape of our own daily reality. The toughest counseling session you can ever have is when someone looks at you and says, "Don't give me any of that guilt stuff. I heard enough of that when I was a kid." Perhaps they did. Professional emissaries of God often overdo it, using guilt as a threat and as a club to beat other people into submission. The Church has almost—but not quite—given guilt a bad name. But without a sense of guilt and an awareness of the fragility of our inner moral equilibrium, we will find it very hard, perhaps impossible, to ever grow in responsibility and in spiritual maturity. I have heard many chilling confessions in my time, but the worst is, "I've got nothing to feel guilty about."

Chesterton's Father Brown is a great teacher of this

painful but necessary truth about faith and detection. "There are two ways of renouncing the devil," he says, "and the difference is perhaps the deepest chasm in modern religion. One is to have a horror of him because he is so far off; and the other is to have it because he is so near. . . . You may think a crime horrible because you could never commit it. I think it horrible because I could commit it."

He goes on in another case to explain his great success in solving mysteries by talking of this close identification with the criminal. An American named Chance calls detection a science when Brown interrupts him to demur. Science, says the priest, allows us to look at the outside of a person, as if he or she were an insect. Placing something under "a dry impartial light" may help us see something factual, but sometimes this light is the reverse of knowledge: "It's treating a friend as a stranger, and pretending that something familiar is really remote and mysterious. . . . Well, what you call 'the secret' is exactly the opposite. I don't try to get outside the man. I try to get inside the man. . . . Indeed, it's much more than that. I am inside the man." Brown goes on to say he tries to actually feel the inner passions, "till I have bent myself into the posture of his hunched and peering hatred; till I see the world with his bloodshot and squinting eyes, looking between the blinkers of his half-witted concentration; looking up the short and sharp perspective of a straight road to a pool of blood. Till I am really a murderer."

"And this is what you call a religious exercise," Chance challenges him.

"Yes," answers Father Brown, "that is what I call a religious exercise."

It is all well and good to say we have empathy for the suffering, and sympathy for those sympathetic—but how do we love our enemies? Perhaps by recognizing that our enemies are already inside us, under our hats, behind our eyes, and silently harboring in our hearts. The mystery story forces us to see this, in the same way that a good spiritual master requires us to seek within. Over and over, the guilty one is the one we least suspect, the paragon of virtue is found to be the very center of sin, and most suspicious of all may even be the detective in disguise. "These are very deep waters," is the phrase Holmes uses to describe this state of affairs and the masks that our affairs can assume.

There is nothing cynical or despairing about this; it is simply a calm, realistic assessment of our true natures, divided, imperfect, shadowed by urges and pain we do not wish the world to see. And to round out the paradox perfectly, sometimes the best way to shield ourselves from this inner shadow is to call it good, and even to parade it as religious virtue. (Reread the parable of the Good Samaritan if you don't believe me; see if this isn't the way it is. The despised one does God's work of simple mercy, and a parade of proud clergy walk by on the opposite side of the street. Who would have suspected it?)

An excellent example of this principle is to be found in Umberto Eco's *The Name of the Rose,* in which the monk Adso (our Watson) tells the dark tale of his friend Sir William of Baskerville's investigation into the disappearance of a book by Aristotle in a labyrinthine library. Along the way we encounter numerous murders, madness, and the fiery destruction of the abbey itself. Eco signals that we are to understand this detecting monk to be a precursor of Holmes, judging by the Baskerville name and the physical description of his sharp eyes, sharper nose, and thin and intelligent face. He even chews tobacco (a three-plug problem). Baskerville employs deduction to solve his problems, much to Adso's wonderment. Eco later wrote that he wanted to write a story that would deliver a metaphysical shudder, and so the form he chose was "the most metaphysical and philosophical: the detective novel." In his hands, the old formula works yet again, and *The Name of the Rose* is probably the best Holmesian tale since Doyle's death.

Eco's monastery is a place of holiness and grace, yet it is also a seething caldron of rage, passion, and murder. Adso observes the monks at prayer, singing the chants: "And hearing this moving harmony, vestibule of the delights of paradise, I asked myself whether the abbey were truly a place of concealed mysteries, of illicit attempts to reveal them, and of grim threats. Because it now seemed to me, on the contrary, the dwelling of sainted men, cenacle of virtue, vessel of learning, ark of prudence, tower of wisdom, domain of meekness, bastion of strength, thurible of sanctity." Holiness is indeed a good hiding place for evil.

The final confrontation with the true murderer and concealer of the prized book is a perfect example of this propensity for evil to perfume itself with sanctity. When confronted by Sir William of Baskerville, the "villain" declares, "You say I am the Devil, but it is not true: I have been the hand of God."

William answers, "The hand of God creates; it does not conceal."

His opponent retorts, "There are boundaries beyond which it is not permitted to go. God decreed that certain papers should bear the words, 'hic sunt leones.' "

"God created monsters, too. And you. And he wants everything to be spoken of."

God has created the detective but also the concealer. The

dark and the light together make the world, and to speak of everything is to pierce the veil of secrets. There in the center of this holy of holies lies the truth: God created monsters—and you. And sometimes they share the same soul. I think this is why Holmes quotes (in German, no less) the words of the great Goethe in *The Sign of Four:* "It's a pity that Nature made only *one* person out of you, for there was material enough for a good man and a rogue." There is nothing like a detective novel to remind all of us of this sometimes uncomfortable fact.

It is said that the most subversive thing that the strict form of the detective novel can do is allow the detective to be the murderer. Think of the uproar when Dame Agatha Christie betrayed the unwritten rules of the game of detection stories in her *Who Murdered Roger Ackroyd?* when the narrator, the Watson figure, is revealed as the killer. Writing about his novel *The Name of the Rose,* Umberto Eco prophesied the truly unthinkable (or is it the inevitable?): "There is still to be written a book in which the murderer is the reader . . . and any true detection should prove that we are the guilty party."

As Father Brown told us, this is a religious exercise.

THE MYSTERY OF *Mysterion*

When reading all sixty Holmes tales, it is a useful reminder of human fallibility that many of the stories are weak and disappointing; for every masterpiece like "The Speckled Band," one has to endure a desultory tale like "The Engineer's Thumb." But even the worst of the stories always offers some special moment of illumination, so that we don't begrudge the fact that pen was put to paper. "The Engineer's Thumb" is illustrative of fallibility in another way, in that Holmes does not succeed in capturing the criminals. In fact, Holmes is not the superman people sometimes imagine him to be, for he often fails, and some of the cases are not even concerned with a legal crime. At least seven times, Holmes comes up short, and this actually improves the series. The omnipotence of later detectives is boring and takes away all true suspense. Doyle, even when he is not firing on all cylinders, always presents us something of sustaining interest, even if it is just a special moment in the fascinating friendship of Watson and Holmes, or just a quote from the Master that redeems the story.

At the close of "The Engineer's Thumb"—after the culprits who cut off his thumb while he hung from a window, making his escape, are long gone—the engineer, Victor Hatherley, remarks ruefully to Holmes, "Well, it has been a pretty business for me! I have lost my thumb and I have lost a fifty-guinea fee, and what have I gained?"

Judging from Holmes's response, he made the right move to become a detective and not a pastor. He actually laughs in Hatherley's face, and replies, "Experience." He adds that the engineer can work it into an excellent story to use the rest of his life.

Experience is the very essence of the mystery of God. By its nature, mystery is resistant to words and images and symbols, and certainly to easy definition. If you want to approach the mystery of God, the gateway is always personal experience. Dermot Lane says it well: "The mystery of God is not some kind of theorem to be proved; it is rather, an experience to be lived."

The novelist Nikos Kazantzakis put it another way.

Once, when he was asked to define God, he told the story of a teacher who said to an almond tree, "Sister, tell me about God."

"And the Almond Tree blossomed."

This experience is something that cannot be given to us, or handed to us, or related to us. It exists and comes into being inside us, as a product of our experiences, circumstances, history, personality, and, as we have just seen, some exposure to the shadow within. In short, I cannot define the mystery of God for you, but I can tell you that you need experience to know it. This is a reality that *we are initiated into.* Even the simple Holmes tales, with their period charm and fantasy, help us to face our own mortality, the fragility of the body, the reality of evil and the shadow of the evil in our own selves. What are we being initiated into? Very simply, to be God's spies.

Many of us would rather have religion come to us in noble philosophical abstractions, drained of all life's juices (tears, blood, sweat)—and clean, shorn of any dirt or smudge of daily reality.

Some of us want religion that is charming and aesthetic, wrapped in a glorious, gorgeous package of angels and calming celestial music, of golden lights and shaded holy spaces.

Some of us want an unchanging creed that effectively removes God from the painful ebb and flow of change, an enshrouded truth that cannot grow and evolve, because this embedded truth is perfect, whole, undivided. And also, by the way, dead.

In stories that, in effect, rip the roof off our lives, God comes *in and through experience,* the ritual and celebration of life's pain as well as its beauty. God is not afraid to get grubby. God has to, to love people. Divine love is in the

grime of my heart as well as the nobility of my intentions. Of course, the great religious teachers have already told us this, but we generally hate to hear it—that sometimes it is the tragic incompleteness within us, this shadow, that brings us back to God.

THE EXPERIENCE OF THE VALLEY OF FEAR

In the grand scheme of things, reading detective fiction probably ranks pretty low on the list of spiritual disciplines, but simply by reminding us of, and returning us to, a proper sense of the realities of our true nature, it certainly redeems itself. For all of its shortcomings, the strangely ritualized form of the detective story—from the opening violent violation of innocence to the last scene of judgment—drenches us in the rawest of experience. David Lehman provocatively says of the reader of these odd mystery/religion texts: "Afflicted as he is with the consciousness of guilt, he may worry that his own sinful secrets will come out, but he's also willing to wager, with suitably crossed fingers, that the Great Detective will absolve him of wrongdoing. And he *is* absolved, at least for the time being. The detective novel has been his confessional." This is a pretty good wager. The God I believe in is actually present in the worst and seemingly impenetrable darkness of our lives. There is an old Jewish story that has an aged peasant saying to his rabbi, "Listen, I have sinned, it is true; but then, God loves to forgive sin. Together, we make a wonderful combination."

We take whatever confessionals we can find. It is somehow reassuring that redemption can come in a ratty, dog-eared old mystery paperback as well as in the glory and grandeur of a gothic cathedral. God is not afraid to be present even in a fiction that wallows in sin.

In "The Illustrious Client," a character named Kitty Winter says of the villain that "He ought to drown in a lower hell than this if there was any justice in the world!" Kitty does not wait for God to dole out this punishment, but inflicts her own retribution in *this* life with the flinging of acid into her tormentor's face. This shocking act causes Sherlock Holmes to exclaim, "The wages of sin, Watson—the wages of sin! Sooner or later it will always come. God knows, there was sin enough."

God knows. God has always suspected. Cain looks up, and awaits the mark upon his forehead that will preserve his life although he is the world's first murderer. This mark, unlike Kitty's savage brand, will warn off those who wish to kill the killer. Though his brother's blood literally cries out to God from the ground exactly who has committed this evil, Cain will live. In fact, as I read the unstated conclusion of the tale, Cain the murderer *must* live, because he is going to father us all.

Sooner or later, sin must come, and come again. The mark of Cain is never completely erased, no matter how much certain religious faiths develop systems and techniques to earnestly try to scrub away the human stain. And overarching all of this is the reality of death. P. D. James, probably the finest detective writer alive, talks about the very strong religious sense in her books, borne of her Church of England upbringing: "I think I was born with this sense of the extraordinary fragility of life and that every moment is lived, really, not under the shadow of death but in the knowledge that this is how it is going to end. So that death is in a sense an ever-present thought. It sounds a little morbid, but I don't see it at all as morbid because I think I'm really a rather happy person who is always aware of this. I think for some people detective fiction does help to exorcise this fear."

Just as Doyle investigated the mystery of death through the seance, we take a sideways look at morality through the detective fable. If detecting made sons of the Devil out of those who wished to rip off the roof of others, imagine what wishing to rip the roof off of death itself makes us! Yet at last it is just this vast blankness of death that draws us into the spell, the exorcism, if you will, of the detective story. We are lured, enticed, to the puzzle parable, as to a mirror.

The main difference between mystery (*mysterion*) in religion and in the common, everyday definition of mystery is this: *mysterion* must be experienced, and cannot be directly communicated. A detective's mystery, on the other hand, can and must be spelled out in words, a neat and ingenious solution to a puzzle. We know that as the story comes to a close, as the pages dwindle to a precious few, that everything will be made clear, lucid, understandable at last. It is as if we wished to make true Emerson's haunting assertion, "Commit a crime, and the world is made of glass."

Yet there is in the mystery story a smoky, hazy hint of this old definition of mystery. In his filmed interviews with Joseph Campbell, Bill Moyers asked the mythologist if what people wanted from religion was eternal truth.

Campbell, who was brimming with energy and charm despite the fact that he was then dying of cancer, replied, "I don't think that's what we're really seeking. I think that what we're seeking is an experience of being alive . . . so that we actually feel the rapture of being alive." Here is a reminder that the mystery religions have not died but are reborn in strange and subtle transformations, again and again. Part of feeling "fully alive" is to experience both the fragility of existence and the reality of sin that dwells even on the gateway to joy and wonder. A chilling moment from the Holmes tales comes when he and Watson are interviewing a woman whose husband has been mysteriously slain, his head blown off by a shotgun blast. Mrs. John Douglas tells Holmes that she thought her husband was harboring some secret, perhaps dating back to his years in America. From listening to him talk she had slowly come to understand that John Douglas was fearful of strangers, of people who might wish to harm him.

"Might I ask," asked Holmes, "what the words were which attracted your attention?"

She answers: "The Valley of Fear. That was the expression he has used when I questioned him. 'I have been in the

Valley of Fear. I am not out of it yet.' " When she asked her husband if they could escape this fear, he would reply that he doubted it was possible.

"Surely you asked him what he meant by the Valley of Fear?" interjected Holmes.

"I did; but his face would become very grave and he would shake his head. 'It is bad enough that one of us should have been in its shadow,' he said. 'Please God it shall never fall upon you!' It was some real valley in which he had lived and in which something terrible had occurred to him, of that I am certain; but I can tell you no more."

Perhaps there are no words to be said. This "Valley of Fear" is more haunting and disturbing, somehow, than the supernatural chills of the previous chapter, because some child of the Devil is behind this all-too-human story. This is a valley we must all visit and be haunted by. We each can pray, "Please God, it shall never fall upon me"; but this is a prayer likely not to be answered—or, as a wag once said, all prayers are answered, but some are answered "No." It is a manifestly real valley, to be sure.

And we are to be its initiates! But we have rituals to help us walk safely and to realize that such experiences are not the heart of the mystery, as real and frightening as they may be. We move on toward the secret that even Mr. Sherlock Holmes can only dimly see.

At last, we come to the place where we must come, up against the wall of mystery, and there is only one way to break through, out of this Valley of Fear. Even Holmes knows there must be something more than logic and reason and rationality. We are at the edge of what can be communicated, at the edge of the shadow. To be one of God's spies means to acknowledge this venture into wonder.

Listen to the Master. Hear the wonder beneath the

despair—even the hope. "What is the meaning of it, Watson?" he asks at the close of "The Cardboard Box." "What object is served by this circle of misery and violence and fear? It must tend to some end, or else our universe is ruled by chance, which is unthinkable. But what end? There is the great standing perennial problem to which human reason is as far from an answer as ever."

But not the human heart.

6 ∗ The Heart of the Mystery

IF REASON is crashing against the wall of mystery, if "the great standing perennial problem" of our fated and fragile lives cannot be brought to successful solution, then what? Perhaps the great detective is overlooking what is most obvious, what is symbolized by the man opposite him who listens; who is roused from sleep with the words "The game's afoot!"; who unhesitatingly risks his life to stand with his friend; and who dutifully records Holmes's words—the humble, the overlooked and underappreciated Dr. John H. Watson. Could it be that the prosaic and mild doctor is part of the opening that Holmes seeks?

The partnership of Holmes and Watson is so firmly established in the stories that we very rarely see one without the other. However, in the middle of *The Hound of the Baskervilles*, Watson has gone, at Holmes's request, to Baskerville Manor to conduct the inquiry without Holmes, and for several chapters the doctor tries as earnestly as he can to follow the examples of detection he has learned from his friend. "I have not lived for years with Sherlock Holmes for nothing," he thinks to himself.

He learns of a mysterious man living on the desolate moors by the ancient stone huts, and he thinks, as he stands at the window and looks out into the bleak night and terrible weather, "It was a wild night indoors, and what must it be in a stone hut upon the moor. What passion of hatred can it be which leads a man to lurk in such a place at such a time! There, in that hut upon the moor, seems to lie the very centre of that problem which has vexed me so sorely." Then he resolves, "I swear that another day shall not have passed before I have done all that man can do to reach the heart of the mystery."

Yes, we are drawn to do all that we can do "to reach the heart of the mystery." This resolution, this desire, is precisely what fuels our search for truth, a truth far greater than merely a figure lurking upon the moor. The stranger there may be revealed as friend or fiend (and indeed, Watson's mysterious man is later revealed to be none other than Holmes himself, there to propel the investigation and protect his friend). The heart of the mystery that reason cannot reach is, for me, revealed in these sixty tales as a revelation of the triumph of friendship over isolation, mercy over justice, and compassion over judgment.

A GLIMPSE OF A GREAT HEART

And that is why Watson is so important. He is not as bright, as incisive, as penetrating, as observant as Holmes, but in so many ways, he is infinitely wiser, and he has as much to teach Holmes as his friend has offered him in forty years of partnership. Indeed, I think it is possible to read this epic of friendship, in eight books totaling over 170,000 words, as a survey of how to make a machine-man into a creature of compassion. Holmes goes through quite an evolution in these stories, and Watson is with him every step of the way, humble, self-effacing, and proving himself over and over again as a partner in the education of the heart.

Watson is not particularly sentimental about Holmes. Indeed, the portrait he offers is so unsparing and incisive that it is a bit of a wonder why he (and by extension, millions of readers across the generations) clearly reveres and idolizes this cold and arrogant being. On the surface, Holmes is not a likely candidate for legendary beloved status. He is aloof, arrogant, addicted to cocaine (at least until he reappears from his long hiatus), and someone who seems to prefer facts to people. In fact, Holmes presents himself as a new kind of scientist, one who likes to work with human beings in crisis rather than chemicals or other physical objects: people are more interesting, as they are more a challenge.

Late in his career, he will refuse food in favor of smoking his pipe: "Because your faculties become refined when you starve them. . . . I am a brain, Watson. The rest of me is a mere appendix." Once he angers the ladies' man in Watson by professing not to notice that a female client was attractive. "You really are an automaton—a calculating machine," Watson cries, for once setting aside his abiding admiration for his strange friend. "There is something positively inhuman in you at times."

Indeed there is. It was years into their association before Watson learns that Holmes even has a brother. "This reticence upon his part had increased the somewhat inhuman effect which he produced upon me, until sometimes I found myself regarding him as an isolated phenomenon, a brain without a heart. . . ." Over and over, Holmes patiently explains that a brain cannot let emotions or feelings get in the way of accurately evaluating the facts of a case. "It biases the judgment," Holmes says of love.

If it is true, as critic Jacques Barzun maintains, that "Detection is par excellence the romance of reason," then Holmes is the ultimate romancer of facts, the man who lives through his reason and his logic. In a genre that worships reason, Holmes, the great brain, bestrides the mystery story like some sort of cerebral god.

In fact, Watson is very clear that unless this brain is properly fed, it grinds to a terrible wreck, and thus thirsts for stimulation of any kind, even drugs. I can well remember, as a young reader of Holmes, growing up in conservative Tennessee and wondering how odd it was that this "children's literature" hero, Sherlock Holmes, was calmly injecting himself with a seven-percent solution of cocaine at the close of *The Sign of Four.* At the time I supposed he could get away with it because his super brain could take it—and besides, the good Dr. Watson would surely somehow save him from himself.

Holmes is less a drug addict than a stimulus addict. Near the beginning of their relationship, he tells Watson plainly that he dreads "the dull routine of existence. I crave mental exaltation." That is why he has set himself up as the world's first and only unaffiliated consulting detective. He did not do it for money or for fame, but to keep the voracious maw of his intellect supplied with fodder. Well into his long career, Holmes was still hovering on the brink of not having enough to think about, and thus regressing back to his cocaine.

Holmes craves mystery, and the more tragic and grotesque the better. He often uses the French term *outré* to describe cases odd and twisted enough to summon all of his powers and gifts. He can even be petty and self-absorbed, blind to others' pain while in the midst of finding the challenge and excitement he desires. In "The Adventure of the Copper Beeches," he even feels sorry for himself that "the days of the great cases are past. Man, at least criminal man, has lost all enterprise and originality. As to my own little practice, it seems to be degenerating into an agency for recovering lost lead pencils and giving advice to young ladies from boarding-schools." At the close of "The Red-Headed League," after a stunningly successful resolution to the case and with praise ringing in his ears, Holmes yawns. "It saved me from ennui." But a moment later he adds, "Alas! I already feel it closing in upon me. My life is spent in one long effort to escape the commonplaces of existence. These little problems help me to do so."

These "little cases" are generally crimes of a high order, often dealing with murder. His smug dismissal of the emotional realities affecting real people is astonishing. These people are important only to keep Holmes from boredom, or worse, self-demolition through the destruction of his own faculties through cocaine.

Even at the best of times, Holmes can be rude and abrasive, especially to the long-suffering and patient Watson. The good doctor sees intimately his friend's egotism, pettiness, and grand self-absorption, but usually is so lost in admiration for Holmes that he dismisses such minor attributes. This changes, however, when Holmes blithely criticizes Watson's writings (which Doyle, with great comic effect and occasional poignancy, loves to insert throughout the stories). Once, after Holmes complains that his friend's case descriptions were too colorful and lively, writer's ego causes anger to well up in Watson.

"It seems to me that I have done you full justice in the matter," he says, thinking to himself at the same time, "I was repelled by the egotism which I had more than once observed to be a strong factor in my friend's singular character."

This is not a simple relationship, and Holmes is not a cardboard-cutout noble detective. He is an odd, brooding character with real faults to go with his virtues. Jeremy Brett, who perfected a cold and idiosyncratic portrayal of Holmes in the well-received British television series, once said, "I was certainly worried at the start about playing this dark, lonely character who never shows any emotion. I was afraid it might even bring my career to a grinding halt." Nor is Watson, despite his reputation as a bit of a gently befuddled buffoon, a simple man. He is brave, dedicated, affectionate, forbearing, and, most importantly, to be Sherlock Holmes's friend, forgiving to the extreme.

As devoted and loyal as Watson is, he is well aware of who he is and what his limitations are. He does not exalt himself or see himself as anything other than being "a whetstone for [Holmes's] mind." In "The Creeping Man," he rather coldly dissects his friend's relationship with himself as being simply a habit, like Holmes's pipe or violin. Watson adds, "I stimulated him. He liked to think aloud in my presence. . . . If I irritated him by a certain methodical slowness in my mentality, that irritation served only to make his own flame-like intuitions and impressions flash up the more vividly and swiftly. Such was my humble role in our alliance." Indeed, when it appears that Holmes is dying, Watson is kept in the dark about his true condition and ruefully admits, "He pushed to an extreme the axiom that the only safe plotter was he who plotted alone. I was nearer to him than anyone else, and yet I was always conscious of the gap between."

Yet there is another side to the story, and it is here that Watson plays his crucial part in the humanizing of Sherlock Holmes. "The gap between," which exists between all friends, lovers, and even God and ourselves, is an abyss that *can* be bridged and *must* be crossed for God's *mysterion* to be fully revealed. One of the most touching and affecting moments in the canon comes at the beginning of *The Sign of Four*, when, desiring to test his friend's abilities to deduce facts from physical objects, Watson hands a watch to him. Holmes hands it back, seemingly defeated by its recent cleaning "which robs me of my most suggestive facts." Still, he ventures a few little tidbits, such as that the watch had belonged to Watson's elder brother, inherited from their father; after which, Watson innocently says, "Anything else?"

"He was a man of untidy habits—very untidy and careless. He was left with good prospects, but he threw away his chances, lived for some time in poverty with occasional short intervals of prosperity, and finally, taking to drink, he died. That is all I can gather."

All of this is true, and Watson rises from his chair to pace, stung with bitter anger at Holmes's calm recital of such painful circumstances. He believes Holmes has used some previous knowledge of his family distress to puff up his talents. "This is unworthy of you, Holmes. I could not have believed that you would have descended to this. . . . It is unkind and, to speak plainly, has a touch of charlatanism in it."

Holmes suddenly realizes how his abilities can wound and hurt. "My dear doctor, pray accept my apologies. Viewing the matter as an abstract problem, I had forgotten how personal and painful a thing it might be to you." Then he mollifies Watson with a detailed description of how the watch bears all the details that reveal this sad tale of his brother. For Holmes, it is always a struggle to get past people's sorrow and distress as anything other than "an abstract problem." Here we can see a glint of light and warmth in Holmes's icy veneer of cold-bloodedness.

Two late stories reveal at last that Holmes's education in human compassion and connection has not been in vain, and, not surprisingly, both tales feature Watson prominently. To test his theory in "The Devil's Foot" that a special and deadly trance poison caused the death of Tregennis, Holmes purposefully exposes the two of them to its effects. Both are quickly put under its horrific spell, and only a superhuman effort by Watson forces them out of the room before two more lives are claimed by the deadly powder. As they lie on the ground while their heads clear, Holmes speaks at last, in a shaky tone, "I owe you both my thanks and an apology. It was an unjustifiable experiment even for one's self, and doubly so for a friend. I am really very sorry." Holmes's arrogance has been shattered.

Watson writes, in a powerful moment in the series, " 'You know,' I answered with some emotion, for I had never seen so much of Holmes' heart before, 'that it is my greatest joy and privilege to help you.' "

This scene is reinforced by one of their last cases, "The Three Garridebs," which in itself is rather slight and hardly top-drawer Doyle, but it contains one of the highlights of the canon. During the final confrontation, the exposed villain suddenly whips out a revolver and fires twice. Watson is shot, "a sudden hot sear as if a red-hot iron had been pressed to my thigh." Suddenly Holmes, after he has first dispatched the criminal with a resounding blow to his head in retaliation, helps the wounded Watson to a chair, crying, "You're not hurt, Watson? For God's sake, say that you are not hurt!"

For me, the next paragraph is the summit of the stories, set like a splendid jewel in an otherwise drab setting. Watson writes:

"It was worth a wound—it was worth many wounds—to know the depth of loyalty and love which lay behind that cold mask. The clear, hard eyes were dimmed for a moment, and the firm lips were shaking. For the one and only time I caught a glimpse of a great heart as well as that of a great brain. All my years of humble but single-minded service culminated in that moment of revelation."

It is a revelation indeed, one that is hard-earned and affecting, precisely because we know just how carefully Holmes has protected himself, nurtured his cold logic and isolation, exactly how he has striven to turn all matters of emotion into abstract calculations. But the "cold mask" is just that, a mask covering an entirely different reality within, and Watson is the only one he trusts enough, in the shock of this moment of fear, to see through to the core. Somehow, all the devotion and the admiration Watson has offered his friend over thirty years is justified in that moment, justified not for another stunning cerebral triumph, but for something so simple, so human—compassion.

We are beginning to discover just exactly who Mr. Sherlock Holmes really is.

A SECRET PASSION FOR MERCY

The first mystery novel for adults I ever read was *The Goodbye Look* by Ross Macdonald, and there is a scene in it that has hung in my consciousness for over thirty years.

Detective Lew Archer is trying to explain his odd choice
of profession. (I wonder how
many ministers could echo
his sentiments?) He says,
"The life is its own reward. I
like to move into people's
lives and then move out
again. Living with one set of
people in one place used to
bore me."

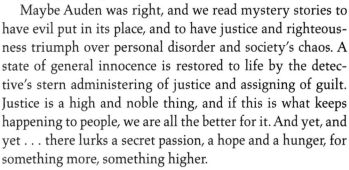

He is immediately chal-
lenged: "That isn't your real
motivation. I know your
type. You have a secret passion for justice. Why don't
you admit it?"

The detective answers, "I
have a secret passion for mercy. But justice is what keeps
happening to people."

Maybe Auden was right, and we read mystery stories to
have evil put in its place, and to have justice and righteous-
ness triumph over personal disorder and society's chaos. A
state of general innocence is restored to life by the detective's stern administering of justice and assigning of guilt.
Justice is a high and noble thing, and if this is what keeps
happening to people, we are all the better for it. And yet, and
yet . . . there lurks a secret passion, a hope and a hunger, for
something more, something higher.

The instances of it may be rare, but detective fiction at its
best can be a spiritual guide to the administration of mercy,
not merely justice. This quality of mercy is another way in

which we can espy the heart of the mystery. Louis Boyer, in his magisterial survey of Christian views of mystery, writes that "the one good news is . . . the heart of the Mystery, an incomparable love, love in its purity, infinite generosity, which exists and subsists only in giving, giving all one has and all one is, culminating in the gift of giving oneself in return." This is beautiful, and true, but sometimes we need to find another way to cut through the grand theological rhetoric, to make this essential truth come alive to us again.

It is the aftermath of Christmas, and Watson, married at the time of "The Blue Carbuncle," has dropped by his old rooms at 221-B to wish his unsentimental friend the compliments of the season. If there ever was a hero less inclined to be drawn into a sweet, mawkish Christmas tableau than Holmes, I don't know who it could be, but in this intriguing and whimsical holiday investigation, even the Master is touched by something powerful. A huge gem called the Blue Carbuncle has been stolen, and only Holmes's brilliant deductions have traced the missing stone to its true thief. Exposed, the man collapses at Holmes's feet, crying, "And now, and now I am myself a branded thief, without ever having touched the wealth for which I sold my character. God help me! God help me!"

Holmes hesitates, then he rises and throws open the door. "Get out!"

"What, sir! Oh, Heaven bless you!"

"No more words. Get out!" And the culprit runs to the street, a free man, a forgiven man.

Calmly reaching for his clay pipe, the detective says to Watson, "I suppose that I am committing a felony, but it is just possible that I am saving a soul. This fellow will not go wrong again; he is too terribly frightened. Send him to jail now, and you make him a jail-bird for life. Besides, it is the season for forgiveness." But Sherlock Holmes does not need it to be Christmastide to offer such mercy. Astonishingly, in fourteen out of sixty recorded cases, Holmes somehow manages to free the guilty, and that does not even count the cases where the hands of justice are thwarted by a suicide, death at sea, or another intervention of providence.

You can make a case that Holmes is an arrogant amateur, interfering with proper administration of the law, that his sense of class superiority to the solidly (and stolidly) middle-class inspectors makes him feel he can toy with people's fates. In "The Abbey Grange," Holmes takes this to the extreme by uncovering the murder of a brutal husband by a noble and unselfish former lover to Lady Brackenstall, and he takes it upon himself to judge the death was by self-defense. In fact, he asks Watson to be the jury, and to conceal the truth from the police. The facts of the crime suppressed, the lovers are free to reunite. "I would rather play tricks with the laws of England than with my own conscience," Holmes blithely explains to Watson.

But this reading of the tales is not adequate or full or fair. Yes, Holmes assumes an unspoken superiority over others that allows him to glide over the law, but that is not the real purpose of his acts of mercy. The heart of the mystery is sometimes not fully revealed in the factual solution to the puzzle but only in the true resolution of the mystery that fuels the puzzle. Justice can be a cruel and unwieldy cudgel if what is needed is the keen blade of a surgeon. Mercy cuts deep and finely, curing with the healer's delicate touch.

This leads us to the next step in discovering the true Holmes. It is a mistake to see him as an adjunct to the police or the justice system. He has another identity entirely, and this identity comes through in the way he chooses to label his profession. He calls himself "the world's first unofficial consulting detective." For a long time, I put the emphasis on the last word of that title, but now it is the word *consulting* that interests me. Doyle always claimed he based his detective on Dr. Joseph Bell, his own medical teacher at the University of Edinburgh. While serving as his outpatient clerk, young Doyle closely observed Bell's uncanny ability to quickly assess not only the patient's disease but also the "occupation and character." Decades later, Doyle recalled how his mentor "would sit in his receiving room with a face like a Red Indian, and diagnose the people as they came in, before they even opened their mouths. He would tell them their symptoms, and even give them details of their past life; and hardly ever would he make a mistake."

It is not surprising that Doyle put so much of himself into his fictional creations. His essential personality lives in the good Dr. Watson; and, likewise, his medical training and what he learned from Dr. Bell he poured into his detective, and Holmes is, at root, a consulting physician, a healer, his Baker Street consulting rooms only blocks away from the famed doctor's consulting offices along Harley Street in London. One suspect who is resisting Holmes's questions even says to him, "You're like a surgeon who wants every symptom before he can give his diagnosis."

"Exactly," Holmes agrees. "That expresses it. And it is only a patient who has an object in deceiving his surgeon who would conceal the facts of the case."

Holmes is not a policeman, nor is he wholly a medical scientist. He holds an odd and uneasy position in relation to all these professions, and the key to his life is found, I believe, in "The Yellow Face," in words he addresses to Mr.

Grant Munro, who stands for all those desperate, heartsick, and lost souls who climb the seventeen stairs to 221-B.

"I was about to say that my friend and I have listened to a good many strange secrets in this room, and that we have had the good fortune to bring peace to many troubled souls." He adds, "I trust that we may do as much for you."

This is the true kind of consulting that Holmes is engaged in, the bringing of peace to people in pain. It is a healing seemingly only he can provide. Thus he is a living paradox, a person who purposely tempers his emotional involvement so as to keep his intelligence hard and keen— but for the purpose of helping, of healing, of revealing the painful and thwarting secrets that twist and maim lives. He is a physician of the soul.

This is why he is so easily moved to release and redeem the guilty, not out of an idle arrogance, but from a deeper sense of his mission to heal, to "bring peace to many troubled souls." At the close of "The Devil's Foot," he faces a man who enacted a terrible revenge on the person who murdered someone he loved. "There is my story, Mr. Holmes," the guilty man says. "Perhaps, if you loved a woman, you would have done as much yourself. At any rate, I am in your hands. You can take what steps you like."

Holmes sits in silence; then, "What are your plans?"

"I had intended to bury myself in central Africa. My work there is but half finished."

"Go and do the other half," says Holmes.

When I read these terse and concise words of liberation, I cannot help but think that very few people have the moral authority to speak such phrases. "Go and sin no more," said one in the ancient past, and the echoes of forgiveness sound on in these parables of mercy. Raymond Chandler, the poet of the hard-boiled detective novel, wrote in his essay "The Simple Art of Murder" some simple words that redeem this largely dismissed genre: "In everything that can be called art, there is a quality of redemption. . . ." We have moved very far from seeing Holmes as a mere calculating machine.

I have often wondered why so many detective novels have featured priests, rabbis, nuns, and ministers, and I think we are close to the answer. Civil authorities reserve their right to judge and to punish, and God bears final authority to forgive or to cast away a soul; but it remains to us, who possess neither judicial nor heavenly power, to do the work of redemption, the human task of reaching out and offering compassion. The heart of the mystery is found as our place in the *mysterion*, the plan that was set before the foundations of the world—and that role is mercy and forgiveness. In Anne Tyler's *Saint Maybe*, a young man's unwise interference in his older brother's marriage has unintentionally resulted in death; shaken, he goes to a minister of an odd little congregation. Burdened by guilt and regret, Ian Bedloe asks Rev. Emmett if, after asking for the people's prayers, he was forgiven. "Goodness, no," the minister says, adding that while God forgives everything, one must offer reparation of a concrete, practical sort, such as raising the three children orphaned by the chain of events Ian had blindly begun.

Shocked, Ian replies he cannot take on the responsibility of three children, that he is only nineteen. "What kind of cockeyed religion is this?"

The minister answers, "It's the religion of complete atonement and complete forgiveness. It's the religion of the Second Chance." This is the religion that Holmes belongs to, the place where forgiveness can enter the resolution of the mystery, a path not of dogmas, but of second chances, love renewed, and mercy above all.

As I read these stirring parables of forgiveness, however, I am troubled by only one thing: that such forgiveness is almost impossible. One Christmas Eve I was called away from my own congregation because my mother's life was threatened. I left the hospital to attend a midnight service, and the minister told a story about a couple he had gone to seminary with whose child had been killed by a young boy on drugs who was driving recklessly. At first, understandably, the couple despised the boy, but through the strength of their faith, they learned to love through the hate and even helped him get off drugs. They forgave the destroyer of their child, and helped save a life; and the boy righted himself.

I remember thinking, sitting by myself in that pew, that I could not have done it. I wasn't big enough, loving enough, to do such a thing. No matter how noble, how inspiring, these parents in the story seemed to live in another realm. And in fact they do. People who forgive like this are not living life as we normally experience it. We look, you and I, for fairness, for justice and justness. When someone hurts us, or betrays us, or treats us with indifference, we respond with hurt, with astonishment, with acute pain and retaliation (the Holmes stories are a catalogue of such responses), and even hate. People who hurt us must pay a price, and we certainly don't want them to prosper, to move on as if our bitter experience did not matter.

Yet when we forgive, when mercy enters the moral equation, we surrender all claim for an eye for an eye, or even simple justice.

What makes forgiveness so hard is that it is counterintuitive. Even Holmes discovered that we cannot reason our way to the feeling, we can't power our way to it, we can't judge our way to it. There's nothing reasonable about it, and thus there is always a quality of the miraculous in people who are merciful. The power of love is never reasonable, and only love makes what *seems impossible* enter this world at all.

What makes this impossible task so vital, so important, is that without it, we are all basically sunk. In a world of justice, we are all in trouble. A world of an eye for an eye, as Gandhi reminded us, produces a world of the blind. Forgiveness is ultimately crucial because we are all so eminently imperfect.

You don't have to wallow in old doctrines like original sin to reckon that the life we share is so constructed that even people of goodwill bump and bruise each other, that our limited perspective and view means that we hurt others unknowingly, that we are forced by circumstances to make tough, sometimes horrendous, choices that wound others; and that, finally, no matter how sincere the rationalizations and justifications, we simply do things that are wrong, that cut deep and betray the very foundations of our lives.

No one escapes this, and we lie to ourselves if we think we do. For something called "light reading," mystery tales do a pretty good job of reminding us who we are. We can gnaw our resentment or guilt like a bone, and grip it as tenaciously as a bulldog. It is a strange kind of spiritual pride to maintain that what we have done, or what others have done to us, is beyond the reach of forgiveness, or God's love (which for me is really saying the same thing). What a bizarre hubris! It is less a question of "forgiving" than one of admitting that we are no longer isolated, no longer cut off from the healing power that is always present and accounted for.

There is an old story of God one day discovering that Heaven is too crowded. It seems everyone has been on the receiving end of divine forbearance. An angel suggests that God owes it to the concept of justice to enforce his laws more strictly. So all are called to stand before the heavenly throne and the angel reads the Ten Commandments. As each commandment is read aloud, it is announced, "All who have broken this commandment will now betake themselves to Hell."

By the time the angel was done, there was only one soul left, a smug, self-satisfied person who had been a recluse in life. God looked down, and said despairingly, "Only one left? I'm lonesome already. All right, come back, everyone!"

At this, hearing that all were forgiven, the recluse bitterly cries out, "This is not justice! And, why wasn't this announced before?"

Opening ourselves to this merciful reality is never easy, but it is an option, and it is the only one that promises anything creative. Loving is reckless, and therefore forgiveness is outrageous; yet it is the only sensible thing to do. If we decide that forgiveness, whether extended to another or to ourselves, is beyond us, we construct an elegant and resilient prison. We resolve to go forth in life carrying the burden, even if it bows us down. Never to forgive leaves the acid of pain to corrode our insides forever, to eat away at us.

We forgive others so we can at last free ourselves from the weight of hate. It is that simple; though simple things are rarely easy.

Learning this takes some consulting with physicians of the heart. It seems that it takes a long career of seeing the worst that people can do to one another, but at last Holmes learns and assumes this inner identity. You might say I am being overly sentimental, which would hardly be appropriate for skeptical Mr. Sherlock Holmes, but I am convinced that Doyle left plenty of clues for us along the way so that this conclusion is inescapable.

The people who are on the receiving end of these acts of mercy stand with Watson in seeing the mask slip to reveal a great heart. Yet we are not just looking at the growth of a cold soul into new warmth and capacity for friendship. We are looking at a quality of soul, of moral greatness, that only the great spiritual teachers possess. By the close of the stories, Holmes has grown so that he becomes less a detective than a confessor figure, a witness to wounded spirits.

The shortest of all the stories contains no deduction at all. In "The Veiled Lodger," Holmes is brought in to hear the story of Eugenia Ronder, who keeps her face always covered in a veil. This tale, among many near the close of the canon, has been dismissed as being a lesser mystery, and this is undeniably true. However, what is often missed here is Doyle's rounding out not only of Holmes's previously stunted and constrained character, but his rounding out of the series. Here there are no tricky clues or stunning conclusions with echoes of "Wonderful, my dear Holmes."

What Mrs. Ronder wishes to tell Holmes and Watson, as her witnesses, is a tragic tale of love thwarted and revenge. As Holmes hears the shocking tale, he sympathetically mutters, "Poor girl! The ways of fate are indeed hard to understand. If there is not some compensation hereafter, then the world is a cruel jest." His typically questioning and dour view of fate is still firmly in place, but empathy and compassion have now assumed primacy.

They learn how the woman's face has been savagely mauled by a lion, and their function of listening to this hard tale completed, they turn to go. Then Holmes makes one of the most important observations of his career.

As Watson tells it, "there was something in the woman's voice which arrested Holmes' attention. He turned swiftly to her."

"Your life is not your own. Keep your hands off of it."

"What use is it to anyone?"

"How can you tell? The example of patient suffering is in itself the most precious of all lessons to an impatient world."

Her response is to Watson "a terrible one." She lifts the veil and exposes the ravages of her torn face. She asks, "I wonder if you would bear it."

With a raised hand of pity, Holmes leaves. Two days later, when Watson comes by Baker Street, Holmes points out to his friend a small blue bottle of prussic acid, a common means of Victorian suicide.

"It came by post," explains Holmes. " 'I send you my temptation. I will follow your advice.' That was the message. I think, Watson, we can guess the name of the brave woman who sent it." By listening, by intuitively sensing her temptation to suicide, and by gazing upon her face, Holmes has helped her reclaim her life as God's, not her own. Instead of solving a murder, Holmes, through this hard-won compassion, has stopped one.

Holmes's gesture when leaving her room, a simple raised hand, takes us back to the roots of the word *mysterion:* to be quiet, to *keep our mouth shut.* Sometimes silence is all we can offer. Gerald Vann wrote: "If you know the love that can lead you near to heartbreak, if you know not only the heights of ecstasy but the depths of pain, then you will know you stand before a mystery and you will be silenced."

A DEEPER DISGUISE

Many years ago, when my wife and I were living in the Midlands of England, one Friday evening we traveled from our home in Birmingham to Coventry Cathedral. I was moved to see the spectacular new cathedral rising up next to the remains of the burned-out shell of the old, leveled by firebombs dropped by German planes in 1942. In the open air of the old nave, hundreds of people had gathered to watch local actors perform medieval mystery plays. Originally produced by medieval trade guilds, these lively plays, which followed the liturgical cycle and were the common folk's version of their faith, were frowned upon by the Church as crude and slightly blasphemous. Actors cavorted where they would have once been banned, with one donning a red Satan's outfit (complete with tail) to tempt a half-clothed couple, shivering in the chill fall air, portraying Adam and Eve. The detective novelist Ross Macdonald once said he enjoyed the slightly shocking and déclassé reputation of the mystery genre, because he believed "the roots of the mystery novel go back to the medieval fabliau, which deliberately dealt with taboo subjects. I think it's significant that very early dramas were known as mysteries. They dealt in a more human way than the Scriptures or church services with sacred subjects and matters of good and evil. Now, of course, what used to be taboo is more or less taken for granted. But a certain aura of evil hangs around the form."

These modern "mystery plays" we call detective stories

are certainly a slight and lively form that few people take very seriously, even the folks who devour each paperback vociferously, like peanuts from a jar. A whiff of the absurd and the scandalous indeed hangs around the form, and it is all too easy to dismiss them as merely frivolous and suited only for the common person. But this is exactly why, like the old mystery plays, theology can be so easily transmitted through them. G. K. Chesterton put it well, maintaining that "The way in which religious mysteries are mixed with merry-making is very shocking to some people—especially . . . to the people who do not believe in religious mysteries."

In looking at human nature, great dramatists have always known the value of "comic relief" in highlighting deep themes. I would submit to you that detective stories are a kind of theological "tragic relief" that highlight God's searching love for this sad, bruised little world we inhabit. God's truth dwells within this taboo form, which exhibits the worst of human nature, and in the figure of the detective who searches for truth and whatever healing is possible in the wrack of human hopes. Wherever redemption is, there is art, and where this design resides, so does God's *mysterion*. The mystery of God has no other place to dwell but in the bright, sad, slightly ludicrous tableau of the mystery of ourselves.

Therein lies our hope; that even when we cry out, like our forefather Cain, that we are not one another's keeper, that God will search us out, sense the evidence of our hearts, spy the signs of our lifeblood spilled to the ground. It is almost as if God needs to wear the disguise of human flesh to know who and what God will be. The Talmud says, "God has no other language than human beings." This is theology enough for me, and why I like mystery stories. Hidden identities are everywhere, and we have to search very hard to see the truth of another's heart. Jesus told his friends that when they fed the hungry, visited the sick, took care of the widowed, and went to the prisons: "When you do this to the least of these, you do this to me." Deeper disguises are everywhere.

Holmes seems to have a particular fondness for donning disguises when he roams through his London to gain the information he needs. Holmes may present himself as a cold, rational person, but there is an extravagant thespian waiting to get out, and it often does. And if we are in search of the deep secrets of the Master, then perhaps it is in the roles he selects that much can be revealed. Oscar Wilde (who was asked to write *The Picture of Dorian Gray* one night at dinner by an editor who then turned to the young doctor next to him and also commissioned a little mystery that would be called *The Sign of Four*) once wrote, "The truths of metaphysics are the truths of masks."

So what disguise does Holmes select when he needs to get into the house of Irene Adler in the first short story? He presents himself to Watson as "an amiable and simple-minded Nonconformist clergyman." Remarks an admiring Watson, "His broad black hat, his baggy trousers, his white tie, his sympathetic smile, and general look of peering and benevolent curiosity" produced an effect greater than merely a change of clothes. "His expression, his manner, his very soul seemed to vary with every fresh part he assumed."

And when Holmes was fleeing the murderous intent of his archenemy Moriarty, he proved his taste in clergyman's gear was not confined to the Protestant. Watson arrives at the train station to meet Holmes so they can escape an increasingly dangerous London, but when the embarkation time for Paris arrives, there is no Holmes. A wave of fear fills Watson, who wonders if something drastic has happened to his friend. To his irritation, a "decrepit" Italian Roman Catholic priest is placed in Watson's carriage. Then, just as his panic begins to crest, there comes a familiar voice:

"My dear Watson, you have not even condescended to say good-morning."

The "aged ecclesiastic" throws off the hat and black cassock, and we are given the clearest picture of Holmes's magic: "For an instant the wrinkles were smoothed away, the nose drew away from the chin, the lower lip ceased to protrude and the mouth to mumble, the dull eyes regained their fire, the drooping figure expanded." That Holmes can time and again fool Watson, who is, after all, a physician and used to close examination, is a remarkable testament to a talent for disguise.

But how interesting that Holmes feels so free to don the garb of men of God!

There is one last disguise, and for once Holmes cannot fault Watson for not seeing through it. For all Watson knows, Holmes has died at Moriarty's hands at the Reichenbach Falls. For three long years, Watson has mourned his remarkable companion, even publishing an anguished account of the death struggle in "The Final Problem." Then, one day, leaving a court where he has heard testimony about a sensational murder (following sensational crimes is now in his blood, a means of preserving something of his lost friendship), Watson accidentally bumps into an old book peddler who spills a book titled *The Origins of Tree Worship* to the ground. When, later in the day, the aged bookman

appears in Watson's office and reveals his identity to the doctor, Watson faints.

Who wouldn't? "Holmes! Is it really you? Can it indeed be that you are alive?"

And the "resurrected" Holmes calmly apologizes for his "unnecessarily dramatic reappearance."

That Doyle delights in this daring disguise is revealed by the shocked disciple confronting what cannot be but is, when Watson replies, "I can hardly believe my eyes. Good Heavens! to think that you—of all men—should be standing in my study. Well, you're not a spirit, anyhow. . . ."

No, standing before Watson is the real flesh-and-blood Holmes, who had been gone, significantly I think, three years in the tomb of silence. How he must have delighted in this greatest disguise of all!

The Gospel of Mark ends its Resurrection account by noting that the women left the empty tomb in "trembling and astonishment"; that "they said nothing to any one, for they were afraid." Watson waits ten years to write his account of Holmes's astonishing return, but nothing can dim or repress his feelings: "Even now, after this long interval, I find myself thrilling as I think of it, and feeling once more that sudden flood of joy, amazement, and incredulity which utterly submerged my mind. . . ."

This can be pressed too far, and Holmes is certainly no Christ, but Watson clearly has had a kind of Easter experience. His faithfulness and devotion have been rewarded in an astonishing and unexpected way, and death has been cheated.

Death may be the ultimate disguise of all, the mask that eternity wears.

Once again, the heart of the mystery is glimpsed in Watson's sound and faithful heart, as well as in the brilliance and spiritual insight of the master detective. Each needs the other, and together, they can help us enter the mysteries as initiates. Van Gogh wrote his brother some words that sum up this important parable of friendship: "One cannot always tell what it is that keeps us shut in, confines us, seems to bury us, but still one feels certain barriers, certain gates, certain walls. . . . Do you know what frees one from this captivity? It is very deep serious affection. Being friends, being brothers, love, that is what opens the prison by supreme power, by some magic force. But without this one remains in prison. There where sympathy is renewed, life is restored."

Still, in the end, Holmes in his complexity and his flawed grandeur remains a mystery we will not easily solve. We learn this at the very beginning of the canon, when Watson is told by his acquaintance Stamford that there is an odd fellow studying at St. Bartholomew's Hospital who is looking for a roommate. After his first meeting with Holmes, he circles back to ask his friend how Holmes seemed to know, to deduce, so much about him at first meeting.

"That's just his little peculiarity. A good many people have wanted to know how he finds things out."

Watson cries out, rubbing his hands, "Oh! a mystery is it?"

Yes. As every human personality is. In Holmes's case, the question is: How can such an egotistic and cool character be yet "the best and wisest man I have ever known," as Watson puts it? We are all gnarled, bent in peculiar places, odd in hidden and not-so-hidden ways. Yet each of us has a deep secret inside us, and each of us is, as Stamford says of Holmes, "a knotty problem."

The heart of the mystery? We all share the mark of Cain, but this mark, pressed in upon our brow, bears nothing less than the loving fingerprint of God.

EPILOGUE * *The Gospel According to Sherlock Holmes*

THE WORD *gospel* means simply "good news." What good news, what joyful proclamations, does detective fiction bring us? I thought of this question when I encountered the parody prayer that the Sherlockian scholar Christopher Morley wrote in the voice of the Great Detective. Part of this heavenly plea goes, "Grant me, O spirit of Reason, matter for Deduction, Intuition, and Analysis; plenty of three-pipe problems. . . . Hold fast the doctrine: When all impossibles are eliminated, what remains, however improbable, must be the Truth. Then, O spirit, be the Game Afoot!"

If Mr. Holmes ever murmured such a prayer while his hansom cab rattled to some murder scene, or as he waited for the spidery, lean figure of Moriarty to climb the winding wet path above the Reichenbach Falls, or while he tended his bees and studied philosophy in retirement, it has never been said. Holmes is not a man accustomed to getting on his knees. But if such Holmesian supplications to the divine are not to come our way, what have we learned?

- That our vision is sound; it is just that we have to train our hearts and minds to notice what we see.
- That religion is found not only in the spectacular but in the simple, the ordinary, the plain and everyday, and that all this is aglow with the mystery of awe.
- That science and spirituality may dwell together in appreciation and wonder of the expanding mystery that the more we know, the more we learn.

•That sometimes it is when God seems farthest away that the invitation to search, explore, and open ourselves to the divine becomes a new and creative beginning.

•That nothing is little, that our lives are more significant than we can know, and that it is often through our pain and guilt that we encounter the hidden God.

•That the Book of Life contains not just judgment and justice, but mercy and forgiveness beyond measure.

These notions will not mollify fundamentalists of any variety—who have God figured out, who prefer God's shroud of mystery torn away at all costs—nor will it satisfy those at the other end of the religious spectrum, who say there is no mystery to reality and that it is all a grand accident of blind force. Either way, they have no time for a mysterious God. But for many of us, this is the only kind of God we can claim as true and real. It may be a frail reed indeed, but I will take my canon where I find it, and rejoice. We have always lived in mystery; it's just that now we are starting to savor it.

Finally, we return to the man leaning against a window shutter (just as we found him at the start of this investigation) contemplating a single moss-rose. "What a lovely thing a rose is!" says Holmes as he falls into a reverie over the flower. "There is nothing in which deduction is so necessary as in religion. It can be built up as an exact science by the reasoner. Our highest assurance of the goodness of Providence seems to me to rest in the flowers."

The lofty thinker lowers his gaze to this object of the earth, this simple coiled collection of crimson petals. The divine is revealed as the ordinary, but there is nothing ordinary in something so beautiful, something that speaks of a power that fuels the very heavens.

A university student goes to the Buddhist teacher Gasan and asks if he has ever read the Gospels. "No, read something to me," the old man replies.

The student opens a Bible and reads from St. Matthew: "And why take ye thought for raiment? Consider the lilies of the field, how they grow. They toil not, neither do they spin, and yet I say unto you that even Solomon in all his glory was not arrayed like one of these. . . . Take therefore no thought for the morrow, for the morrow shall take thought for the things of itself."

Gasan nods. "Whoever uttered those words I consider enlightened."

The student reads on: "Ask and it shall be given you, seek and ye shall find, knock and it shall be opened unto you. For everyone that asketh receiveth, and he that seeketh findeth, and to him that knocketh, it shall be opened."

The old teacher remarks further: "This is excellent. Whoever said that is not far from Buddhahood."

If it is saviors you are looking for or angels you want, you have come to the wrong place. But here is a man who struggles, who uses his brain and in the process discovers his soul, someone who asks us to look carefully at the details of everyday existence as a gateway to mystery. He may or may not be close to Buddhahood (or to sainthood of any sort), but I have come to find him an interesting companion along the spiritual path. He longs for truth, and in the end that is all we can ever hope for, pray for, seek for: the truth revealed in the mystery of God and ourselves.

In the uncertainty of our tangled lives and the secrets we all harbor, there is good news. There is a mystery overarching all, greater and yet more subtle than all that is to our eyes unknown and hidden, and it has existed from before the creation of the world, threaded through its foundations, a surety and an assurance that lies wrapped within a blood-red rose. Such a simple thing.

There is one more disguise, one last view of the seeker.

It comes in the story meant to be the final one, "His Last Bow," in which Holmes emerges from his blissful retirement to aid his country, which is on the verge of a world war. Posing as an American, he has wheedled his way into the spy ring of the German agent Von Bork. At the moment of Von Bork's final triumphant handoff of sensitive British information, Holmes thwarts the German's efforts. Recognizing his true opponent, the defeated Von Bork articulates what so many before him have thought when presented with Holmes's awesome powers: "There is only one man." And to complete the picture, Watson has been posing as the chauffeur, back at his friend's side for one last dangerous adventure.

The saga closes with the two taking a moment overlooking the night ocean to speak of old times. Holmes says, "Stand with me here upon the terrace, for it may be the last quiet talk that we shall ever have."

Pointing to the moonlit sea, Holmes observes, "There's an east wind coming, Watson."

"I think not, Holmes. It is very warm."

Holmes laughs, realizing that the doctor, as usual, has taken his allusion to the imminent great war literally. "Good old Watson! You are the one fixed point in a changing age. There's an east wind coming all the same, such a wind as never blew on England yet. It will be cold and bitter, Watson, and a good many of us may wither before its blast. But it's God's own wind none the less. . . ."

Thus the closing words of Mr. Sherlock Holmes return

us to the unfathomable process of fate and the mystery of a God whose face is hidden from us. Yet this is a fate, as inscrutable and mysterious as it is, that is undeniably part of God's *mysterion,* just as England, in Holmes's final words of trust, will be "cleaner, better, stronger . . . in the sunshine when the storm has cleared."

There are some mysteries you cannot solve.

They must be lived in the raw experience of truth. This is as it must be. The good news is that everyday life, the greatest detective story ever told, happens to be exactly what we have been given. When we are alert, open to what is happening, it is amazing what we can see: everything.

O God, what mysteries I find in thee!
How vast the number of thy purposes!
I try to count them—they are more than the sand;
I wake from my dream,
And I am still lost in thee.

—Psalm 139

FOR NEARLY forty years I have been reading the Sherlock Holmes mysteries, but only recently have I realized that there is a whole world of people obsessed with him who spend their time writing and publishing arcane articles, magazines, Web sites, and novel-length new adventures to praise and pry at what they solemnly call "the canon." Since I am a minister, I have been dealing with a canon all my career—the canon of the Hebrew scriptures and that of the early Christian Church—called the Bible. Thus it was a little odd to start dealing with a whole new canon, but considering that the authorized (i.e., deemed holy and divine) canon comes from a Hebrew word meaning "reed" or "measuring rod," it all made sense. The measuring rod denoted a standard to determine and regulate what is correct and true—a pretty good image for a detective who ferrets out crime, corruption, and lies.

Considering that the last Sherlock Holmes story by Sir Arthur Conan Doyle was written in 1927, Holmes today is in remarkably good shape. He appears in countless movies (in fact, a recent issue of *Entertainment Weekly* crowned Holmes "The Most Portrayed Character" in movie history, with seventy-five actors in 211 movies), television series, and new novels. These portrayals continue to pour out to a voracious audience, as if the continuing best-selling original adventures by Doyle could not possibly be enough to savor or satisfy, even though they run to over 170,000 words in nine books, from 1888's *A Study in Scarlet* to *The Casebook of Sherlock Holmes*—quite an epic in themselves!

Moreover, the potent hawk-nosed image of Sherlock Holmes created by the illustrator Sidney Paget is one of the most instantly recognizable profiles in history, adorning cartoons, advertisements, magazine covers, and even the tiles of the Baker Street Underground station, with Holmes's image composed, when you look closely enough, of hundreds of smaller Holmes profiles. It is hard to escape the master detective.

So you need not be a Sherlock Holmes fanatic to enjoy this book, or be a master of the finer details of this "new" canon. Luckily, the figure of Holmes is so mythic, so ubiquitous, that an easy familiarity is possible for all of us. Indeed, it is why I selected Holmes as the framework of this book about detective fiction and spirituality—no other detective would do.

If by some chance, however, you have not had the pleasure and joy of reading any of the fifty-six short stories and four novels of Sir Arthur Conan Doyle's epic saga of Holmes and Watson, I advise you at least to read the short novel *The Hound of the Baskervilles* and the following ten stories: "The Speckled Band," "The Red-Headed League," "The Blue Carbuncle," "The Musgrave Ritual," "The Final Problem," "The Empty House," "The Second Stain," "The Devil's Foot," "The Problem of Thor Bridge," and "His Last Bow."

Once you sample these, then you can pick and chose other pleasures in the canon; and don't take it as gospel that the later stories are inferior to the early ones, as some critics have suggested over the years. Perhaps as mere puzzles this is true, but one of the hidden joys of the Holmes saga is to be found in the evolution of these wonderful characters across time, from the heart of the Victorian era to the verge of the First World War. And the later Holmes is a more well-rounded, satisfying character, richer in complexity and no mere cold calculating machine.

The best one-volume edition is Doubleday's *The Complete Sherlock Holmes*, the 1927 edition with a charming introduction by Christopher Morley. It has since been reprinted many times, and is therefore easily found in used book stores. Also recommended is the multivolume *The Oxford Sherlock Holmes*, edited by Owen Dudley Edwards (Oxford: Oxford University Press, 1993), which is superb in every regard and contains almost more than anyone would ever want to know about this enduring fictional world, a world that people a hundred years later still want to revisit throughout their own lives, from childhood to beyond.

ACKNOWLEDGMENTS

On a research trip to London on a cold February morning, my son Paul and I stood on Baker Street with friends Dawn Tibbetts and Dermot Walker. In front of the Abbey National Building, we were reading the respectful marker at the place where 221-B, holy of holies for Sherlockians, is supposed to have been. Dermot turned to me and asked, "Stephen, don't you think it is odd that we are visiting an imaginary address of an imaginary person?"

I wish to thank the real people with real addresses who have contributed so much to making this book possible. First, to my wife, Elizabeth, who immediately saw the potential of the idea and encouraged me and tempered me when each approach was needed, my deepest and devoted love. Each of my children assisted in their own way: Paul, in traveling with me on the trail of Holmes in London; Anna, who envisioned this book along with me on our nightly walks; and Elizabeth, who freed up the computer for Dad.

My sincere thanks to my congregation in West Hartford, Connecticut, who have always been supportive, and who responded so readily to the original sermon that started the whole thing. And to my staff—particularly my colleague, Rev. Jean Cook Brown—who always give of themselves, especially during sabbaticals!

To my parishioner Susan Jane Stamm, who helped save the manuscript, and my sanity, numerous times when my computer skills threatened to drag the book down into digital oblivion. (She's also a skilled early editor.) To mentors

Acknowledgments

Forrest Church, George Garrett, Alvord Beardslee, Dan Wakefield, Frederick Buechner, and others, who taught me how to persevere in writing, which can be taught, and for their kindness, which can be caught. For the *Strand* illustrations, I wish to thank the staff of the Hartford Public library, the photographer Ruth Hanks, and my friend Lee Ellenwood for locating them.

Most important, my grateful appreciation to my agent, Flip Brophy, whose support and interest in this and other ideas of mine perfectly defined Saint Paul's definition of faith: belief in things not seen. Her keen enthusiasm and savvy were absolutely irreplaceable. She introduced me to Jane Garrett, whose skill in sculpting a manuscript is always expressed in the most positive manner imaginable. I thank her very much, along with her assistant, Webb Younce. Lastly, without the Solomon-like wisdom of Dan Frank, editorial director of Pantheon, who kindly cut my proposal in half to create two books, none of the above thanks would ever have seen print.

And to the literary skill and spiritual vitality of Sir Arthur Conan Doyle, even if he was ambivalent about having created Mr. Sherlock Holmes. It has been a delight to share in the fictional world he made, and I trust that delight has been transmitted to you, the reader.

(NOTE: Unless otherwise indicated, all citations for quotations from the Sherlock Holmes stories refer to the 1927 one-volume edition, *The Complete Sherlock Holmes,* published in New York by Doubleday.)

Introduction: Spiritual Fingerprints

3   "We reach . . ."   "The Retired Colourman," p. 1,113.
3   "You see . . ."   "A Scandal in Bohemia," p. 162.
3   "It is my business . . ."   "The Speckled Band," p. 254.
3   "abhorrent to his cold . . ."   "A Scandal in Bohemia," p. 161.
3   "These are very deep waters."   "The Speckled Band," p. 263.
4   "a trifle rusty"   "The Crooked Man," p. 422.
4   "Whenever we penetrate . . ."   Albert Schweitzer, quoted in *Treasury of Religious Quotations,* ed. Gerald Tomlinson (Englewood Cliffs: Prentice Hall, 1991), p. 165.
5   "There is nothing . . ."   "The Naval Treaty," p. 455.
6   "Mr. Conan Doyle's hero . . ."   G. K. Chesterton, *The Quotable Chesterton* (Garden City: Image, 1987), p. 323.
7   "I think of slaying Holmes . . ."   Quoted in John Dickson Carr, *The Life of Sir Arthur Conan Doyle* (New York: Harper, 1949), p. 66.
7   "the best and the wisest man . . ."   "The Final Problem," p. 480.
9   "Don't think."   Ludwig Wittgenstein, *Zen to Go,* ed. Jon Winokur (New York: New American, 1989), p. 135.
9   "The foolish reject . . ."   Huang Po, quoted in Steve Hagen, *Buddhism Plain and Simple* (Boston: Tuttle, 1997), p. 148.

Notes

9   "But I have heard . . ."   "The Speckled Band," p. 259.

9   "In over a thousand cases . . ."   "The Final Problem," p. 477.

10   "In one very real sense . . ."   William Davis Spencer, *Mysterium and Mystery* (Ann Arbor: UMI Research, 1989), p. 1.

11   "spend most of their time . . ."   Eugene Peterson, *Take and Read* (Grand Rapids: Eerdmans, 1996), p. 73.

11   "Are you such fools . . ."   The Dragon and Susannah, verse 48.

12   "The mystery's . . ."   P. D. James, quoted in *New York Times Book Review*, Oct. 10, 1982.

13   "When a religion . . ."   C. Day Lewis, "The Detective Story—Why?" in *The Art of the Mystery Story*, ed. Howard Haycroft (New York: Grosset and Dunlap, 1946), p. 399.

13   "Everyday life . . ."   Franz Kafka, in Gustav Janouch, *Conversations with Kafka*, trans. Goronwy Rees, rev. ed. (New York: New Directions, 1971), p. 133. See also David Lehman, *The Perfect Murder* (New York: Free Press, 1989), p. 188.

16   "exceedingly preoccupied . . ."   *The Hound of the Baskervilles*, p. 677.

16   "the sudden death of Cardinal Tosca"   "Black Peter," p. 559.

16   "The Bible!"   *The Valley of Fear*, p. 772.

16   "on miracle plays . . ."   *The Sign of Four*, p. 134.

17   "upon the floor like some strange Buddha . . ."   "The Veiled Lodger," p. 1,097.

17   "amused myself . . ."   "The Empty House," p. 488.

18   "Guard the senses . . ."   *Tao Te Ching*, trans. Gia Fu Feng and Jane English (New York: Vintage, 1972), verse 52.

19   "being the same . . ."   Ibid., verse 1.

19   "policeman of God"   Leonard Holton, quoted in *Mystery Lover's Book of Quotations*, ed. Jane Horning (New York: Mysterious Press, 1988), p. 114.

21   "It is a swamp adder!"   "The Speckled Band," p. 272.

22   "All my childhood stories . . ."   Reynolds Price, *A Common Room* (New York: Atheneum, 1987), pp. 211–13.

22   "Education never ends . . ."   "The Red Circle," p. 907.

23   "What can you gather . . ."   "The Blue Carbuncle," p. 246.

1. The Master's Instructions

24   "I trust that . . ."   "The Red-Headed League," p. 185.

24   "When I hear . . ."   "A Scandal in Bohemia," p. 162.

25   "What is profound . . ."   Charlotte Joko Beck, *Nothing Special* (San Francisco: Harper S.F., 1993), p. 168.

26   "impartial, open . . ."   Mark Epstein, *Thoughts Without a Thinker* (New York: Basic, 1995), p. 126.

26   "The demand . . ."   Abraham Joshua Heschel, *Who Is Man?* (Stanford: Stanford University Press, 1965), p. 116.

27   "Do you know, . . ."   Ernest Bramah, *Best Max Carrados Detective Stories* (New York: Dover, 1972), p. 5.

28   "They say that genius . . ."   *A Study in Scarlet*, p. 31.

28   "To a great mind . . ."   Ibid., p. 43.

28   "genius for minutiae"   *The Sign of Four*, p. 91.

28   "It has long been an axiom . . ."   Ibid., p. 194.

29   To see the World . . .   William Blake, "Auguries of Innocence," from *William Blake*, ed. J. Bronowski (Baltimore: Penguin, 1958), p. 67.

29   "How sweet the morning air . . ."   *The Sign of Four*, p. 121.

30   "A religion to be true . . ."   Doyle, quoted in John Dickson Carr, *The Life of Sir Arthur Conan Doyle* (New York: Harper, 1949), p. 43.

30   "The coat-sleeve . . ."   Carr, *Life of Doyle*, p. 44.

30   "hawk-like amateur detectives"   G. K. Chesterton, "Duties of the Police" in *Collected Works*, vol. 29 (San Francisco: Ignatius, 1988), p. 82.

30   "perfectly graceful . . ."   G. K. Chesterton, *The Quotable Chesterton* (Garden City: Image, 1987), p. 323.

31   "Every stone or flower . . ."   Ibid., p. 188.

31 "What happens in modern . . ." Jacques Barzun, quoted in Robert Paul, *Whatever Happened to Sherlock Holmes* (Carbondale: Southern Illinois University Press, 1991), p. 15.

32 "the little things . . ." "A Case of Identity," p. 196.

33 "The tree was too big . . ." Dan Wakefield, *Returning* (New York: Doubleday, 1988), p. 241.

33 "We see a man . . ." Van Gogh, quoted in Stephen Batchelor, *Awakening in the West* (Berkeley: Parallax, 1994), p. 262.

34 "some sense of the poetry . . ." Chesterton, "A Defence of Detective Stories" in *The Art of the Mystery Story*, ed. Howard Haycroft (New York: Grosset and Dunlap, 1946), pp. 4–5.

35 "Nobody sees a flower . . ." Georgia O'Keefe, quoted in Julia Cameron, *The Artist's Way* (New York: Tarcher/Putnam, 1992), p. 22.

36 "Well, she had a slate-colored . . ." "A Case of Identity," p. 196.

36 "In every tree . . ." Dostoevsky, quoted in *Eternal Quest*, ed. David Manning White (New York: Paragon, 1991), p. 189.

37 "I thought at first . . ." "The Red-Headed League," p. 177.

38 "It is too clear . . ." *The World of Zen*, ed. Nancy Ross (New York: Vintage, 1960), p. 257.

38 "No mask like open truth . . ." William Congreve, quoted in David Lehman, *The Perfect Murder* (New York: Free Press, 1989), p. 83.

38 "there is nothing so unnatural . . ." "A Case of Identity," p. 177.

39 "the capacity to attend" Sarah Coakley, *The Harvard Divinity School Bulletin*, vol. 26, November 1997, p. 7.

40 "that for strange effects . . ." "The Red-Headed League," p. 176.

41 "My dear fellow . . ." "A Case of Identity," p. 190.

41 "It seems, from what I gather . . ." "The Boscombe Valley Mystery," p. 202.

42 "It is a mistake to confound . . ." *A Study in Scarlet*, p. 50.

42 "What is mystery?" Dostoevsky quoted in *Eternal Quest*, ed. White, p. 189.

43 "When you see . . ." Chögyam Trungpa, "Earth and Space," in *Ordinary Magic*, ed. John Welwood (Boston: Shambhala, 1992), p. 28.

43 "I presume nothing." *The Hound of the Baskervilles*, p. 745.

43 "I make a point . . ." "The Reigate Puzzle," p. 407.

44 "If your mind is empty . . ." Ludwig Wittgenstein, *Zen to Go*, ed. Jon Winokur (New York: New American, 1989), p. 125.

44 "Circumstantial evidence is . . ." "The Noble Bachelor," p. 294.

44 "I wish to live . . ." *Hymns for the Celebration of Life*, Unitarian Universalist Association (Boston, 1964), reading 395.

44 "Nature will bear . . ." Henry David Thoreau, *The Winged Life*, ed. Robert Bly (New York: Harper Perennial, 1992), p. 77.

44 "I long ago lost . . ." Ibid., p. 71.

44 "The millions are awake . . ." Ibid., p. 66.

45 "It was a pleasure . . ." Ibid., p. 78.

45 "I thought, Perhaps . . ." *The Journal of Henry David Thoreau*, ed. Bradford Torrey and Francis Allen, vol. XIII (Salt Lake City: Smith, 1984), pp. 73–75.

46 "How often have I said . . ." *The Sign of Four*, p. 111.

46 "It is enough if . . ." Albert Einstein, quoted in *The Mind of God*, ed. Shirley Jones (San Rafael: New World Library, 1994), p. 41.

47 "has paid attention to . . ." *The Letters of Vincent Van Gogh*, ed. Mark Roskill (New York: Quality Paperback, 1991), p. 124.

47 "In your own case . . ." "The Greek Interpreter," p. 435.

48 "I might not have . . . art jargon." *A Study in Scarlet*, p. 36.

48 "Holmes had the impersonal joy . . ." *The Valley of Fear*, p. 773.

48 "Holmes, like all great artists . . ." "Black Peter," p. 559.

48 "Watson insists . . ." *The Valley of Fear*, p. 809.

2. The Case of the Missing God

50 "Did you see him?" "The Retired Colourman," p. 1,113.

51 "I know that He exists" Emily Dickinson, *Complete Poems of Emily Dickinson*, ed. Thomas H. Johnson (Boston: Little, Brown, 1960), P338, p. 160.

53 "Well, it is not for me . . ." "The Boscombe Valley Mystery," p. 217.

54 "Good heavens, Watson . . ." "The Disappearance of Lady Frances Carfax," p. 953.

54 "It becomes a personal issue . . ." "The Five Orange Pips," p. 228.

55 "I don't think . . ." "The Empty House," p. 487.

55 "No riddle is esoteric . . ." Ellery Queen, quoted in *Mystery Lover's Book of Quotations*, ed. Jane Horning (New York: Mysterious Press, 1988), p. 178.

56 "Oh, great." Woody Allen, "Mr. Big," *Getting Even* (New York: Random House, 1972), pp. 102–7.

57 "God disappears . . ." Richard Elliot Friedman, *The Disappearance of God* (Boston: Little, Brown, 1995), p. 3.

57 "It is an ideal setting . . ." Russell Shorto, *Gospel Truth* (New York: Riverhead, 1997), pp. 7, 18.

59 "I am going out now." *The Sign of Four*, p. 97.

59 "You would not think it . . ." Ibid., p. 137.

61 "God is not God's name" Forrester Church, *Everyday Miracles* (New York: Harper and Row, 1988), p. 161.

62 "With the help of . . ." "The Problem of Thor Bridge," p. 1,068.

63 "Only a detective story." Graham Greene, *The Honorary Consul* (New York: Simon and Schuster, 1973), p. 238.

64 "take my assurance . . ." "The Problem of Thor Bridge," p. 1,068.

64 "Some of you rich men . . ." Ibid., p. 1,061.

64 "Well, the stakes are down . . ." Ibid., p. 1,060.

65 "that schoolroom of sorrow . . ." Ibid., p. 1,070.

65 "dazzling obscurity . . ." Dionysius the Areopagite, quoted in *The Treasury of Religious and Spiritual Quotations,* ed. Rebecca Davis and Susan Mesner (Pleasantville: Reader's Digest, 1994), p. 350.

66 "Who shall have it? . . ." T. S. Eliot, *Murder in the Cathedral* (New York: Harcourt Brace, 1935), pp. 28–29.

67 "Whose is it? . . ." "The Musgrave Ritual," in Doyle, *The Memoirs of Sherlock Holmes* (Oxford: Oxford University Press, 1993), p. 123. This quote comes from the English version. American editions contain a slightly different version of the ritual.

69 "All things cover up . . ." Blaise Pascal, quoted in *Eternal Quest,* ed. David Manning White (New York: Paragon, 1991), p. 76.

3. Sherlock Holmes Reads the Book of Life

70 "Have you solved it?" "A Case of Identity," p. 198.

71 "Both the man of science and . . ." Robert Oppenheimer, quoted in *Treasury of Religious Quotations,* ed. Gerald Tomlinson (Englewood Cliffs: Prentice Hall, 1991), p. 351.

71 "a little too scientific . . ." *A Study in Scarlet,* pp. 16–17.

72 "The Book of Life" Ibid., pp. 23–24.

75 "The detective is a prophet . . ." Ellery Queen, quoted in David Lehman, *The Perfect Murder* (New York: Free Press, 1989), p. 13.

75 "Most people, . . ." *A Study in Scarlet,* p. 83.

75 "correctly describe . . ." "The Five Orange Pips," p. 224.

76 "A small beginning . . ." T. H. Huxley, "On a Piece of Chalk" in *English Essays,* ed. Walter Bronson (New York: Henry Holt, 1906), p. 321.

77 "For Inspector Lestrade . . ." Ibid., p. 50.

78 "The whole elaborate . . ." Lehman, *Perfect Murder,* p. 19; see also Roger Callois, "Detective Novel as Game," in

The Poetics of Murder, eds. Glenn Most and William Stowe (New York: HarcourtBraceJovanovitch, 1983), p. 7.

79 "Yes, the beginning . . ."   Peter Ackroyd, *Hawksmoor* (New York: Harper and Row, 1985), pp. 166–67.

80 "He claims that . . ."   *A Study in Scarlet,* p. 37.

81 "No one is happier . . ."   Voltaire, quoted in Harry Eames, *Sleuths, Inc.* (Philadelphia: Lippincott, 1978), p. 5.

81 "the most beautiful thing . . ."   Einstein, quoted in *What a Piece of Work Is Man!* ed. Wesley Camp (Englewood Cliffs: Prentice Hall, 1990), p. 209.

83 "the greatest detective story ever"   Huxley, quoted in Eames, *Sleuths, Inc.,* p. 15.

84 "Now my suspicion is . . ."   J.B.S. Haldane, *Mind,* ed. Shirley Jones (San Rafael: World Library, 1994), p. 13.

86 "Of late I have been tempted . . ."   "The Final Problem," p. 477.

4. No Ghosts Need Apply

87 "Re: Vampires"   "The Sussex Vampires," p. 1,034.

88 "You seem so near the brink . . ."   Robert Richardson, *Henry Thoreau* (Berkeley: University of California Press, 1986), p. 389.

90 "You don't seem quite . . ."   *The Hound of the Baskervilles,* p. 689.

91 "of precise mind"   Ibid., p. 672.

91 "Mr. Holmes, they were . . ."   Ibid., p. 679.

91 "There is a realm . . ."   Ibid., p. 680.

92 "If the devil did desire . . ."   Ibid., p. 684.

94 "looks, in retrospect . . ."   as quoted in Trevor Hall, *Sherlock Holmes and His Creator* (New York: St. Martins, 1977), p. 125.

96 "does not bring doubts . . ."   *Half Century of Chesterton,* ed. D. J. Conlon (Oxford: Oxford University Press, 1987), p. 91.

97 "What we all dread most . . ."   G. K. Chesterton, *The Father Brown Stories* (London: Cassell, 1950), p. 235.

97   "The man was in the maze . . ."   Quoted in Jerry Speir, *Ross Macdonald* (New York: Ungar, 1978), p. 124.

97   "Another part of my trade . . ."   Chesterton, *The Father Brown Stories*, p. 23.

98   "in the last limbo . . ."   Ibid., p. 20.

98   "refers to bafflement of mind . . ."   Gordon Kaufman, *God, Mystery, Diversity* (Minneapolis: Fortress Press, 1996), p. 96.

99   "calls attention to . . ."   Ibid., p. 97.

99   "He truly knows Brahaman . . ."   Quoted in *Treasury of Religious Quotations*, ed. Gerald Tomlinson (Englewood Cliffs: Prentice Hall, 1991), p. 56.

99   "Those who know . . ."   *Tao Te Ching*, trans. Gia Fu Feng and Jane English (New York: Vintage, 1972), verse 52.

100   "But the Almighty law . . ."   Quoted in John Dickson Carr, *The Life of Sir Arthur Conan Doyle* (New York: Harper, 1949), p. 272.

101   "It is devilish, Mr. Holmes . . ."   "The Devil's Foot," p. 958.

101   "I take it . . ."   Ibid., p. 960.

103   "great fierce Irish priest"   *The Quest for Arthur Conan Doyle*, ed. Jon Lellenberg (Carbondale: Southern Illinois University Press, 1987), p. 42.

103   "Is religion the only domain . . ."   Doyle, *The Stark Munro Letters* (Bloomington: Gaslight Publications, 1982), p. 14.

104   "I do not admit . . ."   Quoted in Pierre Norden, *Conan Doyle* (New York: Holt, Rinehart and Winston, 1967), p. 152.

104   "broad Theism"   Ibid., p. 155.

104   "the end and aim . . ."   Ibid., p. 196.

104   "When I add that I am . . ."   Doyle, *The Case For and Against Psychical Belief*, ed. Carl Murchison (Amherst: University of Massachusetts Press, 1927), p. 15.

105   "the science of religion"   Norden, *Conan Doyle*, p. 159.

105   "the first attempt ever made . . ."   Doyle, *Case For and Against*, p. 15.

107 "But there was no stage . . ." From "Introduction" (by Christopher Morley) to Doyle, *The Complete Sherlock Holmes* (New York: Doubleday, 1927), p. 7.

5. God's Spies

109 "And what did you see?" "The Red-Headed League," p. 183.

110 "taking the roof off" Quoted in Ian Ousby, *The Bloodhounds of Heaven* (Cambridge: Harvard, 1976), preface.

111 "The job of the detective . . ." W. H. Auden, "The Guilty Vicarage," in *Detective Fiction*, ed. Robin Winks (Woodstock: Countryman, 1988), p. 21.

112 "So swift, silent . . ." *The Sign of Four*, p. 112.

112 "He is the Napoleon of crime . . ." "The Final Problem," p. 471.

112 "loved to lie . . ." "The Cardboard Box," p. 888.

114 "The deepest and strangest . . ." Quoted in *Treasury of Religious Quotations*, ed. Gerald Tomlinson (Englewood Cliffs: Prentice Hall, 1991), p. 351.

114 "You'll never get . . ." Ellis Peters, *Monk's Hood* (New York: Fawcett Crest, 1980), p. 216.

115 "There are two ways . . ." G. K. Chesterton, *The Father Brown Stories* (London: Cassell, 1950), p. 587.

115 "a dry, impartial light" Ibid., p. 465.

117 "the most metaphysical . . ." Umberto Eco, "Postscript" to *The Name of the Rose* (New York: Harcourt, Brace, 1984), p. 524.

117 "And hearing this . . . harmony . . ." Ibid., p. 102.

117 "You say I am the Devil . . ." Ibid., p. 478.

118 "It's a pity . . ." *The Sign of Four*, p. 115.

118 "There is still to be written . . ." Eco, *Name of the Rose*, p. 535.

119 "Well, it has been . . ." "The Engineer's Thumb," p. 287.

119 "The mystery of God . . ." Quoted in David Regan, *Experience the Mystery* (Collegeville: Liturgical Press, 1994), p. 34.

120   "Sister, tell me . . ."   Nikos Kazantzakis, *Report to Greco* (New York: Simon and Schuster, 1965), p. 8.

122   "Afflicted as he is . . ."   David Lehman, *The Perfect Murder* (New York: Free Press, 1989), p. 30.

122   "He ought to drown . . ."   "The Illustrious Client," p. 989.

122   "The wages of sin . . ."   Ibid., p. 998.

123   "I think I was born . . ."   P. D. James, *The Fatal Art of Entertainment*, ed. Rosemary Herbert (New York: G. K. Hall, 1994), p. 67.

124   "Commit a crime . . ."   Ralph Waldo Emerson, "Compensation," *Essays: First Series* (London: Routledge, 1883), p. 112.

124   "I don't think that's . . ."   Joseph Campbell, *The Power of Myth* (New York: Doubleday, 1988), p. 5.

124   "Might I ask . . ."   *The Valley of Fear*, p. 796.

126   "What is the meaning . . ."   "The Cardboard Box," p. 901.

6. The Heart of the Mystery

128   "I swear that another day . . ."   *The Hound of the Baskervilles*, p. 732.

129   "Because your faculties . . ."   "The Mazarin Stone," p. 1,014.

129   "You really are . . ."   *The Sign of Four*, p. 96.

129   "This reticence . . ."   "The Greek Interpreter," p. 435.

129   "Detection is par excellence . . ."   Jacques Barzun's essay in *Detective Fiction*, ed. Robin Winks (Woodstock: Countryman, 1988), p. 145.

130   "the days of the great cases . . ."   "The Copper Beeches," p. 317.

131   "It saved me from ennui"   "The Red-Headed League," p. 190.

131   "It seems to me . . ."   "The Copper Beeches," p. 317.

132   "I was certainly worried . . ."   Quoted in Peter Haining, *The Television Sherlock Holmes* (London: Virgin, 1991), p. 9.

132   "I stimulated him."   "The Creeping Man," p. 1,071.

132   "He pushed to an extreme . . ."   "The Illustrious Client,"
p. 994.

133   "which robs me . . ."   *The Sign of Four,* pp. 92–93.

134   "I owe you . . ."   "The Devil's Foot," p. 965.

134   "a sudden hot sear . . ."   "The Three Garridebs," p. 1,053.

136   "The life is . . ."   Ross Macdonald, *The Goodbye Look*
(New York: Knopf, 1969), p. 127.

137   "the one good news is . . ."   Louis Bouyer, *The Christian
Mystery* (Petersham: St. Bede's, 1990), p. 293.

137   "And now, and now . . ."   "The Blue Carbuncle," p. 257.

138   "I would rather play tricks . . ."   "The Abbey Grange,"
p. 646.

139   "would sit in his . . ."   Trevor Hall, *Sherlock Holmes and
His Creator* (New York: St. Martin's, 1977), pp. 78–79.

139   "You're like a surgeon . . ."   "The Problem of Thor
Bridge," p. 1,060.

140   "I was about to say . . ."   "The Yellow Face," p. 353.

140   "There is my story . . ."   "The Devil's Foot," p. 970.

141   "In everything that can . . ."   Raymond Chandler, "The
Simple Art of Murder" in *The Fatal Art of Entertainment,*
ed. Rosemary Herbert (New York: G. K. Hall, 1994), p. 237.

141   "Goodness, no"   Anne Tyler, *Saint Maybe* (New York:
Knopf, 1991), pp. 122–23.

144   "Only one left?"   A version of this story, "The Pharisee,"
can be found in Anthony de Mello, *The Song of the Bird*
(New York: Doubleday, 1984), p. 121.

145   "Poor girl!"   "The Veiled Lodger," p. 1,101.

146   "If you know the love . . ."   *Treasury of Religious Quotations,* ed. Gerald Tomlinson (Englewood Cliffs: Prentice
Hall, 1991), p. 352.

147   "the roots of the mystery novel . . ."   Quoted in Jerry
Speir, *Ross Macdonald* (New York: Ungar, 1978), p. 107.

148   "The way in which . . ."   *More Quotable Chesterton,* eds.
George Martin, Richard Rabatin, and John Swan (San
Francisco: Ignatius, 1988), p. 413.

149   "The truths of metaphysics . . ."   Oscar Wilde, *The Works
of Oscar Wilde* (London: Spring, 1963), p. 91.

149 "an amiable and simple-minded . . ." "A Scandal in Bohemia," p. 170.

150 "My dear Watson . . ." "The Final Problem," p. 475.

151 "Holmes! Is it really you?" "The Empty House," p. 486.

152 "Even now, after . . ." Ibid., p. 483.

152 "One cannot always tell . . ." *The Letters of Vincent Van Gogh*, ed. Mark Roskill (New York: Quality Paperback, 1991), p. 126.

152 "That's just his . . ." *A Study in Scarlet*, p. 19.

Epilogue: The Gospel According to Sherlock Holmes

154 "Grant me, O spirit . . ." Christopher Morley, *The Standard Doyle Company* (New York: Fordham University Press, 1990), p. 215.

156 "No, read something . . ." *The Gospel According to Zen*, eds. Robert Sohl, Audrey Carr (New York: New American Press, 1970), p. 39.

157 "Stand with me here . . ." "His Last Bow," p. 980.

(NOTE: "SH" stands for "Sherlock Holmes." Arthur Conan Doyle's stories and books are listed under their titles. Other authors' works are listed under those authors' names. Fictional characters are listed under their surnames.)

Index

Index

"The Great Cloud of Unknowing," 83

"The Greek Interpreter" (Doyle), 47

Greene, Graham, *The Honorary Consul*, 63–64

Gregson (fictional character), 28

guilt:
  and detective stories, 136
  as necessary spiritual tool, 113–15, 122, 155
  sense of, in detective stories, 112–15

Hadrian, 62

Haldane, J. B. S., 84

Harris, Deborah Turner, Sir Adam Sinclair "Adept" series, 93–94

Hassidic story, 32

Hatherley, Victor (fictional character), 119

healing, guilt and, 113–15

Hebrew scriptures, 57

Heisenberg's uncertainty principle, 83

Heschel, Abraham Joshua, 26, 39

Hinayana Buddhism, 16–17

"His Last Bow" (Doyle), 157, 162

Holmes, Mycroft (fictional character), 18

Holmes, Sherlock (fictional character):
  admiration of W. Reade philosophy, 59–61
  biblical references made by, 21–22
  character based on that of Dr. Joseph Bell, Doyle's teacher, 139
  cold, egotistic nature of, 129, 131–34
  craving for stimulation and mystery, 130–31
  "death" of, 7–8, 17–19, 55, 150–51
  deep, true, hidden nature of, 135, 138–40, 145–46, 149, 153
  disguises of, 149–51
  as Doyle's alter ego, 106, 139
  drug habit of, 18, 129, 130
  duality of evil and grace in, 112–13
  evolution of character of, in course of stories, 128–29, 132–35, 145–46
  family heritage of, 47–48
  forgiveness of, 145
  great-chain-of-life idea, 72–86
  as legend, 6, 8
  lessons on compassion learned from Watson, 133–35
  melancholy of, 50–51, 53–54
  mercy delivered by, 137–38, 140–41
  modern media portrayals of, 161
  moral stature of, 9

Index